ISBN 978-1-332-03325-6
PIBN 10272867

This book is a reproduction of an important historical work. Forgotten Books uses
state-of-the-art technology to digitally reconstruct the work, preserving the original format
whilst repairing imperfections present in the aged copy. In rare cases, an imperfection in
the original, such as a blemish or missing page, may be replicated in our edition. We do,
however, repair the vast majority of imperfections successfully; any imperfections that
remain are intentionally left to preserve the state of such historical works.

For support please visit www.forgottenbooks.com

1 MONTH OF
FREE
READING

at

www.ForgottenBooks.com

By purchasing this book you are eligible for one month membership to ForgottenBooks.com, giving you unlimited access to our entire collection of over 700,000 titles via our web site and mobile apps.

To claim your free month visit:
www.forgottenbooks.com/free272867

RIFLES AND RIFLE SHOOTING

BY

CHARLES ASKINS

AUTHOR OF "THE AMERICAN SHOTGUN"
"WING AND TRAP SHOOTING," ETC.

Illustrated with Diagrams

NEW YORK
THE MACMILLAN COMPANY
1919

FOREWORD

THE sword, the lance, the longbow, and the long rifle were the weapons of romance. The sword has been a practically useless arm all these three hundred years, yet it is carried by military men and others simply because of its tremendous hold upon the imagination. The knight and his war-horse, his lance and his great two-handed sword are alive to-day, just as they were a thousand years ago, though his immense blade has dwindled in modern hands to a mere toy to be carried on parade—for four hundred years popular imagination has kept it hung to the soldier's waist after its work was done.

If we are a nation of riflemen to-day, it is not because the nation needs us for its defense, not from military ardor, but for the reason that the American boy is trailing in the footsteps of a lean lanky figure, clad in homespun and leather, across his shoulders the long rifle that never missed. This man of the woods, the plains, and the mountains, iron-like, aquiline, aggressive, unafraid, with a weapon as deadly as death, is still trailing the dark woods, and following him are all the youth of America who know American tradition. Hence are we a nation of riflemen who shoot the arm for its own sake and for the beloved tradition connected with it.

English history has its longbow, France, its sword, Normandy, its axe, but American romance has only the rifle. It fed the children of the pioneer, conquered his enemies, made life bearable. Deep in his heart, where dwell vanity and pride, the descendant of the backwoodsman believes that the American is the only real rifleman to-day, and the only one that ever will be.

Then let the romancers romance! Long live Cooper and Leather-stocking! Even Wild Bill and the James boys will do more good dead than they ever did harm alive if they lead our youth to shoot a rifle and shoot it straight. Let us raise more English sparrows, and jay birds, and neighbor's cats for the small boy to shoot at, since he needs them in his business of training to become a rifleman.

CHARLES ASKINS.

Ames, Okla., February, 1912.

CONTENTS

CONTENTS

CHAPTER I

THE American breechloading rifle in a practical form dates from the closing years of the Civil War. Previous to that time many models of breechloaders had been invented, and some were being manufactured in an experimental way, but they had attracted little attention. However, the needs of a great war could not fail to stimulate mechanical ingenuity to the utmost, and the result was that while many freak weapons were produced, others were of such sterling design that in a modified form they are in use to this day. At the close of the Rebellion certain regiments of our troops were armed with Henry, Sharps, and Spencer rifles, the two former making a great reputation for themselves as sporting weapons in the succeeding years.

The manufacture of the Spencer rifle was early discontinued and no description of that arm seems necessary here. The Sharps and the

RIFLES AND RIFLE SHOOTING

Henry, however, developed side by side, and for many years divided the popular approval of the American sporting public.

Neither of these weapons was ever used by the army to any great extent subsequent to the War, for the military service soon adopted a special weapon of its own, but big game hunters were quick to see the advantages of a breechloading mechanism with its fixed ammunition, and in a very few years such arms had entirely replaced every description of muzzleloader.

The Sharps was a single shot, the Henry a lever-action repeater. The former might be considered the parent of all the single-shot rifles made on the falling breech-block principle including the Ballard, Remington, Winchester single-shot, Stevens, Martini-Peabody, and several models made in England to-day.

There is no better single-shot action at the present time than the old Sharps-Borchardt hammerless with a falling breech-block, finger lever, kicking extractor, and block so shaped at the top that the cartridge would slide home with its own weight. After it was modeled the English war rifle and other European military arms in use up to the date of nitro powders. Why this arm was rejected by our own authorities in favor of the old Springfield .45 is one of the mysteries that only a board of military experts could explain.

The Sharps, together with its rivals, the Winchester, Ballard, and Remington single-shots, was instrumental in developing all our most powerful black powder cartridges. For two or three decades following the Civil War the single-shot was the preferred arm of hunters simply because cartridges of greater power than could be used in any repeating rifle of the time were adapted to it.

Powerful long range and express ammunition was manufactured for these rifles, ammunition of a kind now all but obsolete. The .44-100-520 Sharps and the .45-100-550 Sharps made long distance sharpshooting records that can scarcely be excelled to-day, besides being used effectively upon the buffalo and grizzly bear. These cartridges were loaded with both patched and lubricated bullets, the former being preferred for match shooting. Later the Winchester Company remodeled the .45-100, loading it with more powder and less lead. It then showed a very flat trajectory for a black powder rifle and plenty of killing power, but was never so well liked as the old long range cartridges owing to excessive fouling and lack of accuracy for any great number of shots.

RIFLES AND RIFLE SHOOTING

The Henry rifle was the progenitor of our present lever-action repeaters the Winchester, Marlin, Savage, Stevens, and some other makes like the Colt and Bullard, now discontinued. In the beginning repeating rifles used rim fire ammunition of very moderate power and range, but gradually these arms were chambered for center fire cartridges of greater strength, and with such charges they began to replace the single-shot for big game shooting. At the time when nitro powder began to supersede the black some very fine black powder cartridges were made for these rifles, and the arms were thought to be as good as anything that would ever be required for big game. However, the charcoal powders have seen their day, and possibly the style of rifle that used them will presently disappear.

The single-shot and lever-action repeaters will be treated more at length under their proper heading, for they still retain all their old time popularity for certain purposes. Some of the models, like the Sharps, Ballard, Remington, Maynard, Springfield, .45, Bullard, and Colts have become obsolete, however, and will require little further mention. The "Old" Springfield, by the way, was an arm differing in mechanism from anything that preceded or followed it, a weapon capable of splendid service, as witness many " good " Indians buried all over the Western plains. It was replaced by the Krag-Jorgensen, previous to the Spanish-American war, though the National Guard were still armed with it up to the beginning of this century.

Another black powder rifle that came into existence during the decades between 1880 and 1900 was the pump-action repeater. As a black powder arm, using heavy hunting cartridges, it was never very well liked, but with miniature ammunition the model has always enjoyed a high degree of popularity.

Nitro powder and the military organizations of the world are responsible for the appearance of the bolt-action repeating rifle which made its debut in the early nineties. Military exigencies demanded, first, a repeating rifle in place of the single shot once in common use; next, a reduction in caliber with the consequent lessened weight of ammunition; third, a far higher velocity and flatter trajectory than was possible with black powder.

The result was a general rearming of civilized nations with the bolt-action, .30 caliber repeater. This arm fought the Russo-Japanese war and has met every military requirement, but is not likely to see service again in a contest of such magnitude. Our own weapon of war, the New Springfield, belongs to this type of arm, and its good qualities and defects as a hunting rifle will be mentioned in their proper places.

The heavy, double express rifle is the preferred arm of big game hunters in Asia and Africa. Since an increasing number of American sportsmen are now shooting in those countries this weapon is entitled to a due amount of space in a volume devoted to sporting arms, even though few of them are built in America or used here. The double rifle is the most powerful hunting arm made.

Three barrel guns, consisting of two shotgun tubes with a rifle barrel lying beneath, are well adapted to hunting purposes under certain conditions, as where small game abounds together with large game of a non-dangerous character. The use of this gun has always been limited with us, however, and they are now in less demand than formerly. The same can be said of the gun and rifle combination, one rifle and one shotgun barrel, and of the double barrels which are rifled only at the muzzle, permitting the shooting of both loose shot and ball from one tube.

The decade between 1900 and 1910 must be

credited with the most modern type of rifle, and the one that bids fair to replace all others in course of time—the automatic or self-loader. Of these we have three models, all differing essentially in mechanical principle but every one a weapon of merit. All the gun inventive genius of the world is now turned to the perfecting of an automatic rifle in which both the soldier and the sportsman are equally interested. At present self-loading arms are not thought to be simple enough in mechanism to withstand the exacting demands of hard campaigning, but the nations of the world are waiting for them.

Just now America leads in automatic firearms, but what a year will bring forth no one can tell. Germany is destined, probably, to take a leading part in the development of military selfloading rifles.

CHAPTER II

THE SINGLE-SHOT RIFLE

THE single-shot rifle has by no means outlived its usefulness. I think it a safe statement to say that as many cartridges are now fired from single-shot rifles as from all other models combined. For certain purposes, as where there is no necessity for rapidity of fire, the single-shot can never be excelled by any repeater. Its days as a military arm are over, and few American hunters would carry it to the woods, but after all is said, not many bullets in each million fired are directed at a man or animal. From which it may be inferred that the great virtue of the single-shot rifle lies in its furthering the admirable American propensity for shooting at some kind of an inanimate mark.

The single rifle accomplished its share of game killing in times gone by. The Remington and Sharps " needle guns " were the preferred weapons of the buffalo hunters and mountain men

18

of the West. Renowned hunters like Paul du
Chaillieu and Sir Samuel Baker staked their lives
on a single huge, round bullet of four or eight
bore. Even now the single-shot will usually be
found in the outfit of a big game hunter of Asia
or Africa. But for us, we have relegated it to
the art of scientific or miscellaneous rifle practice.

Though a number of makes of once highly
esteemed single-shot rifles have been discontinued,
it is still manufactured in this country and
Europe in a large variety of styles. We have the
falling breech block and finger lever; the drop
down barrel, lug bolted and actuated by top or
side lever, also the military bolt action, besides
a miscellaneous lot of bolting mechanisms chiefly
found on cheap imported arms.

The English have adopted the American finger
lever and falling breech block, also a modification
of the old Sharps in their Martini-Peabody, yet
the shotgun style of breech fastening, a top lever
and drop-down barrel, has always been the most
popular with them. They have both black and
nitro powder rifles with this fastening for the
most powerful cartridges that have ever been
used in shoulder guns. Lug bolted English rifles
have been made in all calibers up to a four bore
shooting sixteen drams of powder and a bullet

weighing over eighteen hundred grains. Nevertheless, despite their partiality for the shotgun mechanism in the rifle, they have found it wise to adapt the breech block to their high pressure cordite weapons.

Our riflemen have never been very friendly to the lug bolt and drop-down barrel, though a number of such arms were made in this country at one time. The trouble with this style of rifle is that the barrel will loosen with wear, and then, if the sight is on the tang, inaccurate shooting must follow. Anyway no man would care to shoot a shaky rifle in these days of high pressure charges.

While other mechanisms, like the military breech bolt, have merit for use on a single-shot, nevertheless the writer is convinced that all single-shot rifles should be made with the falling breech block. This action has all the merit of every other, and many good points which none of the rest possess. The heavy breech block of solid steel, wedging in behind the cartridge, is absolutely indestructible, and no accident with it is possible except actually splitting open the frame of the gun. Such a falling block mechanism as that of the Sharps, Winchester single-shot, or that used by Jeffery and Greener in England should bear double the bursting strain of the best nickel steel rifle barrel ever made. In fact, one frame with its locking block can be expected to outwear a dozen barrels,—might be considered, in truth, indestructible unless allowed to rust out.

The further advantages of the falling breech block rifle is that the barrel can be made either rigid or take-down, the one being as sound and serviceable as the other. The beauty of the take-down lies in the facility with which barrels can be made to interchange on one action. The .32--40, .38-55, and other barrels having like size of cartridge head can all be used on one frame. The Stevens people even made a rim fire .22 to interchange with their center fire barrels.

The single-shot is the one arm really adapted to such refinements of rifle manipulation as set-triggers, telescope and other fine rifle sights, variations in powder and lead, bullets seated ahead of shell from breech or muzzle, and other contrivances tending to the greatest accuracy both of sighting and bullet flight.

As a consequence, except in military work, the single-shot is the chosen arm of the match shooter, whether his work is accomplished off-hand or at rest, at long or short range. Even in military match shooting there is little doubt but that the single-shot would be the preferred arm if Government regulations did not forbid it. In the old days of black powder and big bores no repeater could hold its own with the single-shot, and I see no reason to believe that they could to-day, notwithstanding our New Springfield has been pronounced the most accurate long range rifle in existence.

There are more reasons for the preference accorded the single-shot by match shooters than need be dwelt upon here. Among them is a closer fitting shell chamber which insures the bullet centering in the bore. Additionally this style of rifle permits a wide variation in barrel lengths and weights. As a rule the smokeless powder repeater has a light barrel limited in length. On the other hand, the single-shot can be had with number one to number five barrels, in length from twenty-four to thirty-four inches varying in weight from three to ten pounds. For target shooting, either at gallery distance or two hundred yards, no other rifle than the single-shot receives much consideration.

Single-shot rifles are made in many styles from the two and a half pound pocket rifle to the sixteen pound Schuetzen gun. I have seen target rifles the naked barrel of which weighed twelve pounds. In Europe this style of aim is chambered for all the heaviest hunting cartridges, including the .600 bore cordite intended exclusively for elephants and weighing nearly twenty pounds. The favorite gallery rifle tips the scale between nine and twelve pounds, the sharpshooter's piece from eleven to fifteen, the small game hunter's arm from five to eight.

Stocks can be had of every description, straight grip, pistol grip, rifle butt, shotgun butt, Swiss butt, Schuetzen butt, and cheek pieces of different shapes and designs. Many of the stocks are handmade to satisfy individual fancies and demands. Even the style of the lever is varied to suit the taste; it may be the ordinary curved finger lever, a loop lever, such as repeating rifles have, or some one of the many Schuetzen levers.

Of all gun men the match shooter has the largest stock of whims and cranky notions; the average sharpshooter will not be satisfied with anything a factory can turn out, but must exert his individual ingenuity in finishing up his rifle. A visit to a rifle range will demonstrate that hardly any two of the participants will be satisfied with even the same description of butt-plate.

The single-shot rifle must always be the chosen arm of the rifle crank, the man who shoots a great deal and who is fond of experimenting with gun and ammunition, perhaps firing a thousand shots at various targets to one at a living object.

While the single-shot rifles have been chambered for nearly every cartridge that has ever been built, yet in this country we might now safely limit the arm to calibers from .38-55 down to .22 short. The most appreciated sizes will be the cheap rim fires, .22 and .25, and such center fires as can be readily and cheaply reloaded, like the .38-55, .32-40, .28-30, .25-25, .25-21, and .25-20.

The center fire cartridges named can be charged with either black, semi-smokeless, or smokeless powder, with bullets of soft lead or metal patch. Barrels can be obtained of the ordinary tensile strength or of nickel steel, guaranteed to withstand heavy pressure and high velocities. Altogether the " student " of rifle shooting shows his wisdom in a partiality for the single-shot rifle.

CHAPTER III

THE LEVER-ACTION REPEATER

THE lever-action repeater is so familiar to every American who shoots a rifle that a description of its mechanism is uncalled for. It has been in use in this country without radical change of design for over forty years, and for over three decades has been the favorite big game rifle of the American continent. Many have been exported to all parts of the world except Europe. It has speed of fire, strength, endurance, reliability, and power.

This model of rifle, like the single-shot, is an American invention and is now the only type of rifle built exclusively in the United States. Doubtless a majority of our people would have preferred seeing it adopted by the army. That it was not selected for this purpose was not due to any inherent fault of the arm, especially for sporting purposes, but because a first class hunting rifle may have but moderate utility as a soldier's weapon.

The under lever is well adapted to sure and rapid functioning in any position a hunter is likely to assume, but is inconvenient to manipulate from the favorite military prone position. Further, lever-action rifles cannot be clip loaded, the tubular magazine of the old models was not adapted to pointed bullets, and the mechanism cannot be dismounted and cleaned without the use of tools. All of which considerations are of moment in military service.

Speed of fire must be considered of a great deal more importance to a big game hunter than the ability to manipulate the arm readily from the prone position, while clips are practically useless to the hunter who will either down his quarry with the supply of cartridges in his magazine or shoot until it has escaped, in either case having plenty of time to reload. Speed of fire is absolutely essential in a modern sporting rifle where the arm is frequently used in the woods or at running game which may be in sight but two or three seconds. The American hunter is particularly fond of an arm which repeats rapidly with a good reserve in his magazine, since, being " shotgun trained " for the most part, he is apt to be quick on the trigger rather than sure of his aim. If every man could be a graduate in still hunting, doubtless a single shot would do, but the average big game shot must take his chances, running, standing, or flying, making amends for lack of stalking skill by accurate and rapid fire.

A word here as to the rapidity of fire of the different types of sporting rifles mentioned in this volume: I should estimate that the automatic is twice as fast as the pump-action, the pump will fire three shots to two with the under lever, and since the latter can be functioned without removal from the shoulder, it is doubly as quick (in the hands of the average hunter) as the military bolt. The single shot is not to be considered as a big game rifle because it is too slow. The double barrel is, of course, as fast as any for the two shots it carries, but the man who uses this arm should follow the usual custom of having a gunbearer with a spare weapon within easy reach.

Naturally the above is not taking into consideration the effect of recoil upon the gunner which might be so severe as to make him practically as fast with one gun as another. Where the weapon has a free recoil of near a hundred pounds no man is going to fire it twice in a second. Familiarity with one action and not with another would make a difference also, as would the man behind the gun, but these are unknown factors which cannot be considered.

Reliability of functioning is an absolute requirement in a rifle intended for such game as might become dangerous. If there is a possibility of a shell sticking, or the arm balking once in a hundred shots it should be rejected, for a man's life might depend upon that hundredth shot. A grizzly or a moose, not to mention African game, needs only one uninterrupted charge and his work is done—and so is the hunter's. The lever-action is one of the most reliable rifles ever constructed. If the rifle is kept in any sort of condition with ammunition that has never been reloaded, there is no possibility of a shell sticking. It is yanked out with a long lever that can pry like a handspike and the same power replaces a spent cartridge with a loaded one. Speed of fire, reliability, accuracy, and power sufficiently account for the prestige of this type of arm among American hunters.

Some of the criticisms of the lever-action are rather of the hair-splitting order, but in fairness I must give them. The Briton finds fault with it as being noisy. His evident conclusion is that a man must go about through the woods working the lever and alarming game. However, as to this I can see no reason for the marksman to manipulate his lever except when actually firing, and then the explosion of the cartridges would surely make noise enough to drown the clicking of the lever.

Probably the fairest criticism of the action is that it cannot be dismounted or cleaned without the use of tools, and that sand and foul weather are more liable to disable it than the single-shot, double rifle, or the military bolt-action. Whatever truth there may be in this, it is certain that this rifle has gone through various campaigns in India, Africa, and the Arctic regions without occasioning its users a particle of trouble. Indeed it must be admitted by anyone who has given rifled fire arms sufficient study that there is more real gun value, at the cost, in a standard lever-action rifle than in any other rifled arm in the world.

As a rule, lever-action rifles have a tubular magazine, either full or half length, lying under the barrel, but one model of this arm is made with a box magazine, and another has one that revolves like the cylinder of a revolver. Which should be selected is much a matter of individual preference, governed, too, by the cartridge to be fired. The box or the revolving magazine should be chosen where cartridges are to be used having sharp-pointed bullets, since in a tubular magazine, the sharp point might cause an accident through coming in contact with the preceding shell.

Theoretically the box magazine should further balance and handiness, because the weight of ammunition is carried midway between the two hands which support the piece. However, this is merely theoretical, for in practice, I, at least, much prefer a rifle that does not balance like a shotgun, but hangs rather heavily at the muzzle. A rifle having a comparatively heavy barrel, which means muzzle heavy, can not only be held steadier in the off-hand position, but the direction of the bullet is also less affected by the jump and flip of the barrel. Extremely light weight and shotgun balance in a rifle are snares for the unwary, unless the piece is of the very smallest caliber or is used exclusively for snap and running shots.

The lever-action rifle can be had either with rigid barrel or take-down, the hunter usually preferring the latter and the scientific rifleman the former. The take-down is said to shoot loose with excessive use, but not one sportsman in a hundred will ever give it that much service, and it is certainly more convenient to clean and to pack away for transportation.

When smokeless powder military cartridges were first designed, it was supposed that only the single-shot or the bolt-action rifles had sufficient strength to withstand the tremendous pressures, but experience has proved this conclusion wrong, for the lever-action repeaters are now chambered for the most powerful cartridges manufactured in America.

While these rifles have been cut for a large variety of cartridges, ranging from .22 to .50 caliber, yet since the model and mechanism of the arm is such that it is difficult to manufacture it in light weights, we now find the piece practically limited to big game cartridges. Few would select a lever-action rifle for any cartridge smaller than the .25-35-117, preferring the pump-action for anything lighter. However, high-power hunting cartridges are adapted to it in such variety that it seems the most exacting demands ought to be satisfied. No matter what game is intended to be pursued, from woodchuck to grizzly bear, a rifle and cartridge can be obtained perfectly designed for the work in hand.

The lever-action repeater should now be considered as a high-power rifle only. All the numbers of black powder cartridges for which it was once chambered might now be regarded as quite obsolete, and the low pressure smokeless ammunition which replaced them should be viewed in the same light.

CHAPTER IV

THE PUMP-ACTION REPEATER AND THE MILITARY
BOLT-ACTION

THE mechanism of the pump-action is the same as that of the well-known repeating shotgun—a sliding forearm that ejects and reloads by means of a straight pull back and forth. Formerly this type of hunting rifle was chambered for many sizes of hunting cartridges, but in a day when hand reloaded ammunition was common, with the expanded and tight shells that followed as a matter of course, the straight pull lacked leverage in ejecting and reloading. For this reason, with the exception of the Standard rifle and the Marlin, manufacturers have been content to make the pump action arms in .22 caliber only. The Marlin Company is building a rifle in .25-20 and the Standard has gone still farther in turning out weapons in calibers from .25 to .35 high power with this action.

Pump-action rifles are generally built in light

32

weight, from four and a half to six pounds, and are therefore, not especially designed for range and gallery, though very accurate and capable of making good scores. Its light weight, balance, rapidity, and general handiness make it the chosen weapon of the rifle snapshot, the man who prefers to use his weapon shotgun fashion, striking his mark while it is in motion. For small game, too, and as a companionable outdoor piece it is a prime favorite.

The Colt Fire Arms Company was the pioneer in pump-action rifles, but has long since given up their manufacture. There might be a reason for this other than any inherent defect in the arms since that firm is very completely occupied in turning out revolvers and automatic pistols, nevertheless the impression remains that the action was not a success where large game and heavy cartridges were concerned.

The Colt rifles were deceptive in this way: Try out one in a gun store or upon the range and it appeared to work perfectly, but in practical service, in game shooting, the owner would be balked by it every now and then at a critical moment. The trouble is partly the inability to make a human being into a good working machine; under excitement he does things hurriedly and ineffectively, or what he then accomplishes must be of a very simple nature. I have never yet seen a man with a pump-action gun, either rifle or shotgun, that was not balked by it occasionally. This matters nothing with small game, only one opportunity gone in a large number, but with big game that one lost chance might utterly spoil an outing. Of course with dangerous beasts it would be foolhardy to select a weapon that could jam or balk.

Notwithstanding this, I am inclined to believe that using the clean, smokeless powder ammunition, and never attempting to reload a cartridge, the mechanism would be quite satisfactory with certain high power loads, like the .25-35 and .30-30, certainly it works perfectly in calibers up to .25-20.

The whole question is merely one of leverage, for the action is faster than that of any other hand-operated repeating rifle. If equally reliable, it would be chosen in preference to the lever or the bolt-action. It is simpler than an automatic, has cleaner lines, can be made lighter in weight, and in the hands of an expert is rapid enough for any practical purpose, but it is a question if it can ever be made non-balkable. On the whole, in these days of rapidly developing auto-loaders and increasing power and breech pressure, we may fairly conclude that the pump-action will always be limited to small game and miniature cartridges.

BOLT-ACTION RIFLES

The bolt-action, usually termed the military bolt, is by no means the modern invention that many suppose, the mechanism of the arm being in fact a gradual evolution, as is true of other styles of rifles. The patents of Dreyse, of Prussia, issued in 1838, contain the first idea of the breech bolt, his patents practically covering the needle gun adopted by the Prussian army in 1842. The American patents of Hall & Day, dated 1839, were the beginning of the bolt in this country; in principle their gun was the same as that of the Prussian. The Winchester Company began building a weapon of the bolt-action type in 1878 which they termed the Hotchkiss. It had the magazine located in the stock after the fashion of the Spencer, and was a neater appearing gun in consequence than the present box magazine Springfield, but never became popular, being finally abandoned.

Game hunters in this country paid little attention to the bolt-action until it was adopted by the United States army in the shape of the foreign Krag-Jorgensen some time in the early nineties. Even subsequent to this period the weapon was comparatively unknown outside of military circles. With the coming of the New Springfield, however, and the revival of target practice by the National Guard, this type of arm began to appeal to hunters as well as soldiers. The improvement of the .30-40 ammunition in 1903 and 1906 led to the further popularity of the gun and charge.

At present the military action threatens to become a fad among hunters, something readily accounted for. The modern Springfield is a sterling piece of work, and so wide is the interest in military shooting at this time that many sportsmen are affiliated with the militia, hence from preference carrying their familiar weapon into the woods. Moreover the New Springfield and similar rifles have undoubted merit as sporting weapons. The advantages of the Springfield are: it is one of the most accurate rifles made; its trajectory is the flattest of American rifles; it is powerful enough for the largest of our game; the piece will bear more rough usage than other styles of repeating rifle, being almost proof against rust and sand; the mechanism can be dismounted for inspection and cleaning without the use of any tool, while the gun is compact and of about the right weight for a hunter's weapon.

The military slingstrap of this arm is the correct thing for carrying a rifle, besides being a positive advantage in off-hand shooting. The Springfield, too, is made of better than ordinary material, and, under certain restrictions it is sold by the Government to individuals at very moderate prices, about one-third of what would be asked for a similar arm built in Europe.

Of late the army Springfields are being remodeled by private gunsmiths in accordance with the lines preferred by sportsman, the weapon restocked with fancy wood, pistol grips hand-checkered with reduced length of fore-end, and so on. Thus altered, the arm is as handsomely designed a rifle as can be found anywhere, while at the same time the weight has been materially reduced. The Springfield was used in Africa by Roosevelt with much success, and other Americans, now hunting on that continent, are following his lead. Some go so far as to maintain that this weapon and its cartridge are powerful enough for any African game, but they are misled by a limited experience and over-enthusiasm.

RIFLES AND RIFLE SHOOTING

Notwithstanding the truth of what has been said above, I doubt if the bolt-action is the correct thing for the average hunter, especially if he has become accustomed to a faster mechanism. The bolt is decidedly slow since the hand must be removed from the grip to catch and work it, and most men will need to drop the butt from the shoulder in doing this. Then the motions in ejecting and reloading are complicated; first the bolt-handle has to be raised and then drawn back, shoved forward, and again turned down to original position. It is conceivable that circumstances might arise which would make a faster action extremely desirable. Greener says that the bolt-action is too slow for charging game, animals certain to fight, like lions and tigers.

Moreover, while it is admitted that the bolt guns are superior when it is a question of long range and an extended " danger zone," as the military have it, yet I believe that the old principle that an extremely long range rifle is not needed for game shooting still holds. Ninety-nine per cent of American game is killed at distances under three hundred yards, and no sacrifice of other essentials should be made in order to acquire an arm that is especially qualified for work at a thousand.

PUMP-ACTION REPEATER

Among English and Continental sportsmen the bolt rifle is displacing the double barrel to quite an extent, but at this time, in Europe, the tendency is to discard the .256 and .303 in favor of larger bores like the .333 and .404. The velocities of these last named cartridges range from 2,200 to 2,600 feet; the bullets weigh from 250 to 400 grains, and the striking force of either is about two tons—double that of the .30-40-220. I need hardly add that such weapons are unnecessarily powerful for any game we have, with the possible exception of Alaska bear, while the recoil in a light bolt gun is very severe. The matter of recoil in proportion to weight of arm will be mentioned later on.

To sum up the case of the bolt-action rifle, the arm is strong, reliable, accurate, high in velocity, flat in trajectory, chambered for the most powerful ammunition in use in a repeating rifle, but *the weapon is slow*. Few would consider it adapted to use in the woods or for running shots.

CHAPTER V

THE double express rifle has never been in much demand in this country, but any American who has occasion to shoot in India or Africa will find it wise to include one or more of these weapons in his armory. Men who hunt game of the nature of elephants, rhinos, lions, and tigers, have long pinned their faith to the double rifle, and we have no grounds for disputing their good judgment. Perhaps in course of time some form of magazine rifle will replace the double express, but up to the present date no other weapon has been found quite so deadly and reliable upon a charging beast at close quarters. More emphatically is this true where the English manner of stalking is followed, with the sportsman carrying one rifle and his shikari the second. If any rifle ever supersedes the double it seems now that it must be an automatic.

THE DOUBLE RIFLE

The highly finished English double rifle has long been considered the finest example of the art of gun building. Beyond question it requires more gunsmith's skill to put together two rifled tubes and insure that they will shoot to the same center at all distances from short range to the maximum than to construct any other style of gun. Not every double rifle will do this either, and the sportsman who finds himself in need of one of these arms should purchase only from the very best maker, and even then should carefully target and test his weapon.

The trouble with the double rifle is that both barrels may not shoot on exactly the same elevation, or they may shoot apart, or cross their missiles. Indeed it is quite impossible to make double rifles quite as accurate at all ranges as a single barrel, but for practical purposes, at sporting ranges, they are just as effective.

There is no disputing the claim that a double hammerless, self-ejecting rifle of high grade is a splendid weapon. It is quicker with its two shots than any repeating rifle with the exception of the automatic; there is no such thing as balking or jamming it for the two shots it contains, whatever the excitement, and the arm is chambered for the most powerful sporting cartridges in use.

Rifles of this description, when constructed of moderate weights to use medium cartridges, should have much the feel and balance of a shotgun which especially fits them for the sort of instinctive snap work that must sometimes stop a charging beast.

Double rifles can be obtained suitable for shooting any species of game from rooks and rabbits to elephants, in weights from five pounds to twenty. If it were worth while to purchase one of these weapons for American shooting, the .333 as made by Jeffery, using a 250 grain bullet driven with a velocity of 2,600 feet should certainly prove a killer. This cartridge is more powerful than anything we have and might appeal to the man who is looking for striking force and deadliness.

For service in India and Africa the double rifle can be obtained in various bores and cartridges. Some of the best liked are the .375, .400, .404, .450, .475, .500, .577, and .600 cordite. The latter is charged with one hundred grains of powder and a nine hundred grain bullet and is warranted to kill anything before it—perhaps behind as well.

No less an authority than W. W. Greener maintains that the recoil of these great rifles is unbearable, and that they never should have been built in such calibers. Probably the best double rifles for African game would be the .333, .400, .450, and .475. They appear to be quite powerful enough for elephants, have velocities and trajectories equal to the ordinary military small bores, and the recoil is to be preferred to the swing of an elephant's trunk.

In purchasing a double rifle economy should not be considered. A first rate rifle can hardly be secured under three hundred dollars and five hundred might well be expended for one. These rifles are made after the same design as the ordinary double shotgun by some builders, hammerless, ejector locks, top lever, and single trigger, where desired. The most favored mechanism for the more powerful cartridges, however, is the under lever, in which the lever which withdraws the lug bolts lies under the guard. It is stated that the under lever has ten times the withdrawing force at the top and that it entirely obviates jams from the tremendous pressure which sometimes occurs and disables the gun temporarily where the top lever is in use. The one excuse for the great double express rifle is its *danger* and it would not do to add to this by a mechanism that might possibly render the weapon useless in a time of peril.

RIFLES AND RIFLE SHOOTING

THE SHOTGUN AND RIFLE

Double barrel guns with one barrel for shot and the other rifled have never been manufactured in America so far as the writer is aware. Some of them have been imported, chiefly in the hands of immigrants from Germany and France. I think not a great many of them are now being made even in Europe.

This sort of weapon has its uses in a country of mixed small and large game. It is well adapted to driven deer shooting after the German fashion especially for small deer like the roe. One barrel loaded with buckshot could then be used for running animals and the rifle cartridge for still shots. The arm once saw a certain amount of service in the south where chasing deer with hounds, heading them off, and shooting from horseback was the accepted style. It is a handy gun for mixed turkey and small game, but for this purpose is not so good as the next model we have to consider, the three-barrel.

THE THREE BARREL GUN

The three-barrel gun as now constructed has two shotgun barrels lying side by side as usual

44

with a rifle barrel beneath. But two locks are used to fire the three barrels, the shift being made from one of the shot barrels to the rifle by means of a lever. These weapons are still being built in this country, also numbers of them are imported.

Formerly they were manufactured in different styles, some with the rifle barrel on top in place of the top rib, and the late D. Kirkwood, of Boston, has made them with four barrels two shot and two rifle. He was an old time expert gunsmith of a kind now becoming rare.

The three-barrel gun is an attractive arm for certain purposes. For the mixed shooting such as can be found in Florida or Texas, principally quail and wildfowl but occasionally deer or turkey, it is a combination not to be excelled in a single weapon. It is, of course, a good double shotgun with the added advantage of an accurate rifle always at the sportsman's command. In a country like Texas, Mexico, or Central America where the game may be turkey, deer, bobcats, wildfowl, or quail, I do not know of a more useful weapon than the three barrel.

These arms are now being chambered for modern high power cartridges such as the .25-35, .30-30, .32-40, and .38-55, as well as for lighter ammunition, including the .25-20-86. Probably the .30-30 is the most favored cartridge, with 16 or 20 gauge shot barrels, the entire arm to weigh not exceeding 7¼ pounds.

Even the man who shoots in a well settled country can get quite a bit of sport out of his three barrel that he would otherwise miss. With it crows, hawks, foxes, and woodchucks can be killed, while it is a more sportsmanlike weapon for shooting rabbits and squirrels than any shotgun. Cracking the head of a squirrel in the top of a hundred foot hickory is a worthy feat, but shooting him with shot is mere pot hunting.

The use of a three-barreled arm is pretty well confined to America, North and South. In Europe a different weapon replaces it, the muzzle rifled shotgun.

As its name implies, this is a shotgun with its muzzle having a shallow rifling, calculated to spin a cylindrical, pointed bullet of moderate length. Usually the ball is hollow at point or base, sometimes both, so as to permit the greatest length of missile without undue weight.

The most popular sizes of " ball-and-shotguns " are the 20 and 28 gauges. The 28 drives a rifle bullet of 290 grains, the 20, one of 380. The velocities are from fourteen to sixteen hundred feet, and the striking force from seventeen hundred to twenty-four hundred foot pounds. The accuracy is said to be nearly equal to a double rifle at ranges up to two hundred yards. The arm weighs in these lighter gauges from 5¼ to 7 pounds. With a shot charge the weapon is about as effective as any other cylinder bored gun.

Arms of this description would no doubt be very convenient where the sportsman was obliged to travel light, as in long canoe voyages, where the limit of weight was one gun, and the game of a mixed character. As a rifle the power would be sufficient for anything up to moose.

The rifled shotgun is also made in heavier bores, 16, 12, 10, and 8, with charges running as high as ten drams of powder and a thousand grain ball. While such weapons are used in India for cover shooting there is little about them to attract an American sportsman.

CHAPTER VI

IT seems a foregone conclusion that the rifle
of the future must be automatic in its reloading. Sportsmen and military authorities are so nearly unanimous about this that their
very expectations would force the development
of the arm. Doubtless the first type of rifle that
the automatic will entirely replace will be the
army gun of all countries. Sporting rifles will
follow gradually, for in the nature of things they
cannot be changed so suddenly or radically. The
last of our present models to give way should be
the single-shot and the double barrel—the one because a self-loader cannot improve upon a single-
shot where rapidity of fire is useless while the
double rifle of large bore will have a special field
of its own so long as the great game of Asia and
Africa remains.

It is not to be expected that men will continue
to pump a gun, yank a lever, or push, pull, and
twist a bolt when the rifle can be made to do it

all more uniformly and more quickly and surely. Conservatism and caution will of course have an effect for a time, which is the history of firearms from the beginning. Self-loading is in its youth; changes will be made and improvements are sure to come. Perhaps in course of time we will come to look upon our present automatics as extremely crude.

However, since the self-loader is about the only model of rifle that hasn't reached full development, we can expect the gun inventive ability of the world to be turned solely in its direction, with certain and gratifying results sure to follow. While the careful man may consider it wise to bide his time and await the gun of the future, I cannot forbear a word of praise for our automatics just as they are.

I am free to admit an honest liking for an automatic. No grizzly ever charged me yet, but if he should I want to hit him once for every jump he makes, and twice while he is falling,— all this without a thought to the rifle further than to hold and pull trigger. If a repeating rifle is needed at all, the demand should be for the one that repeats the quickest, with the least effort of mind and muscle on the part of the marksman.

RIFLES AND RIFLE SHOOTING

For the novice whose first shot may not mean sudden death, for use in the woods where a vital part of the animal may not even be exposed, for running shots, there is no rifled firearm to compare with an automatic. Critics may complain that this model looks clumsy compared with its highly developed rivals, that its mechanism is complicated with too many springs, pieces, and parts, nevertheless I believe that every make of these rifles is strong, reliable, compact, and exactly adapted to the work required of it. I have yet to hear of the unprejudiced man who was dissatisfied with one of these weapons after giving it a fair trial, or of one of them that failed to give a good account of itself in a hot corner.

There are two or three points wherein I think the rifles could be improved, though for mechanical reasons the changes may be difficult. The barrels are now made twenty and twenty-two inches, while the man who likes a long sighting plane would prefer them longer. Moreover in one of the models the trigger pull is hard and drags, which is of course a detriment to good rifle work. Further there is a demand for higher velocity ammunition than anything now used in an automatic, and this may be expected to have a bearing on future models of the rifles. The three makes of these rifles we now have differ materially in self-loading principle, and one or the other will finally prove its superiority, I have little doubt.

The Winchester Company constructed the first of these rifles, a .22 caliber, and their next two larger models were of inferior power, range, and trajectory, giving the impression that under their reloading principle it was impossible to make automatic arms up to modern requirements. However, the latest arm of this company, the .401 proved this conclusion erroneous, for it can be considered a nearly ideal big game cartridge, with an initial velocity approaching 2,200 feet, trajectory of less than six inches, and striking force of more than a ton. Doubtless should there be a demand for it the arm will be adapted to ammunition of still higher power because larger bores with increased bullet energy would entail little if any greater breech pressure than the cartridges now in use.

The ammunition of the Winchester automatic rifles, .351 and .401, is a positive advance in cartridge making. They are loaded with a condensed powder which, while giving full velocity, permits a shorter shell, and in turn a shorter frame, lessened weight of action, and other advantages. I see no reason why this sort of powder should not replace the bulkier kinds in other rifles, because it is compact and cheaper, while giving as regular and high velocity with no increase in breech pressure. If a cartridge two inches long will do the work of one of three inches, what is the use of carrying about the increased amount of metal?

The Remington-U. M. C. Company has chambered their auto-loading rifle for cartridges that are all good big game loads, calibers being from .25 to .35. The .35 is similar in ballistic properties to the .401 Winchester, though not loaded with the same powder. Sighted and shot at two hundred yards, it has accuracy and flat trajectory sufficient to keep the ball in a six inch circle anywhere along its curve of flight. It strikes nearly a two thousand pound blow, and the diameter of the ball is such as to insure upset on impact and good execution. Other cartridges for which the Remington is bored are the .25-35,-117, 30-30,-170, and .32 Remington special all being rimless.

The third model of the auto-loading, the Standard, is novel in that the same gun will function either automatically or by hand with the trombone action—the change necessary being made in a few minutes. This rifle is chambered for the same ammunition as the Remington.

Mechanically our three automatic rifles differ. In the Winchester the barrel is rigid, and the breech bolt is opened by what is known technically as the " blow-back " action; the bolt is not locked but is held in place by the inertia of a recoil block backed by a heavy spring. The Remington has a barrel which slides inside a steel jacket. Under pressure of the charge the barrel moves back, still locked to the breech bolt, until the bullet is out of the muzzle, then the barrel comes in contact with a lug which stops it while the bolt continues rearward, opening the breech, ejecting the spent shell, and reloading through the action of a compressed spiral spring.

The Standard is known as a " gas-operated " rifle. In it the breech bolt is actuated by the powder gas which is taken into the power-tube, lying under the barrel, through a small port near the muzzle. No gas can be taken into the power tube until the bullet has passed the port, so the action remains locked until the bullet has cleared the gun. In changing the gun to a hand functioned arm the port is closed and some other slight changes made.

All of these rifles in question have box magazines. The Winchester and Remington can be clip loaded or the cartridges forced into the magazine one at a time. The Standard has a hinged lid at the bottom of the magazine and to reload it you have simply to open the lid and drop the cartridges in, the only care needed, being to see that the bullet end is turned in the right direction. Either of the three guns can readily be used as a single loader.

The things that concern a hunter relative to his rifle are that it must be reliable, accurate, speedy, possess killing power, and have a mechanism that can withstand hard usage. Beyond question any self-loader is more complicated than a single-shot, and whether any of them will last a lifetime is more than I can say, though I suspect that any one of these guns which receives ordinary care will live long enough to become obsolete through later improvements.

While America seems destined to lead in automatic firearms, rifles, pistols, or shotguns, yet European countries are at present very active in their experiments with weapons of this sort. As is to be expected, nations with large standing armies and little game are more interested in strictly military arms than those intended for sport. Germany now has one regiment armed with automatics, and that is only a hint of what is coming.

The average American is a gun crank from childhood, but it must be confessed that he gives more thought to his own individual plans and to his hunting weapons than to the guns carried by Uncle Sam's army. As a consequence we find our sporting arms always well to the front with the military trailing the procession. This is not true at this writing, however, and the New Springfield should do very well, until the lads of blue and khaki actually once more need a gun to shoot at somebody with.

Perhaps I may be forgiven for speculating somewhat idly here, at the close of this chapter on the rifle which the immediate future is to bring forth. To begin with, the most of us will readily admit that it is to be auto-loading. A majority would vote for a weight of between seven and eight pounds for a hunting arm, with a barrel length of about twenty-six inches.

The caliber will vary between .280 and .350. Cartridges should be loaded with condensed powder and consequently be less bulky than those we have now. Barrels will be made harder, of greater tensile strength, and bullet jackets should be so improved as to do away with metallic fouling. Three thousand feet a second will be accepted as the standard muzzle velocity, and many cartridges will exceed it—even now an experimental rifle has been built which gives a muzzle velocity of 3,500 feet.

Despite the increased velocity, no greater breech pressures will be engendered, for the manufacturers of nitro powder are keeping even step with the procession. Accuracy will be improved over all ranges, and the military marksmen will extend their long range to a mile. In army rifles the short bullet, such as the Springfield .150 and the Ross .139 will be dropped for lack of ranging qualities.

The standard muzzle energy for an American big game rifle will be from 2,500 to 3,000 feet pounds. Steel will be so treated chemically as absolutely to prevent rusting. For a given energy of bullet, recoil will be considerably reduced. Some form of silencer might be built in with the rifle in place of being a separate piece.

CHAPTER VII

RIFLE CARTRIDGES

Miniature and Gallery.—Small Game.—Matd ɪ
Rifle,—Military and Sporting, No. 1. M´li-
tary and Sporting, No. 2.—Large Bore, H_gh-
Power Cartridges.

THE choice of a proper rifle cartridge for
the work in view is of the highest 'mport-
ance. A sporting writer has aptly stated
the matter when he says that the rifle itself is a
mere means of using the cartridge and is, in fact,
of secondary importance. Hence it s that at
least in the hunting field our success ɪ ay be due
in a greater measure to the cartridge selected
than to the model of rifle. Dozens of cartridges
are still being manufactured for rifles that are
either obsolete or should be. It follows that the
novice may go astray even when he consults a
veteran friend who may be clinging to what was
good in its day but is now out of date.

Ammunition firms divide cartridges into black

powder and smokeless, most of the black powder output being also loaded with some brand of nitro. Smokeless shells in turn are subdivided into low-pressure and high-power. The former is simply the old black shell loaded with a brand of nitro giving practically the same ballistics as the original charge, while the latter are either cartridges that have never been designed for anything but smokeless or the old shell loaded with a high velocity powder.

While thousands of black powder shells are still manufactured and will be until the guns for which they are built are worn out, yet we can consider black powder for big game shooting as obsolete. Very few men, indeed, would deliberately choose a black powder rifle and cartridge for hunting purposes, to-day, even for small game. I shall, therefore, in this work pay little attention to the old line of black powder game shells that were once well liked, but have outlived their usefulness. The one purpose for which our old friend saltpeter is still as well adapted as any is target shooting, gallery and match rifle. It is peculiarly fitted to arms from which thousands of shots are fired in the course of a season, because the wear on a barrel is very slight compared with nitro compounds and the

RIFLE CARTRIDGES

necessarily jacketed bullets. While smokeless powders have been so perfected as to show accuracy and regularity equal to black powder, yet their wear and tear on a barrel will make many chary of using them in a fine match rifle.

The low pressure smokeless, such as is used to replace the black, is a makeshift, and like any other makeshift must in the nature of things be temporary. Another decade should witness the end of all the old-time black powder cartridges, the low pressure nitros, and the big game rifles in which they are used. Even the made-over cartridges, those that have been changed to high velocity like the .38-35, .40-70, 45-90, and .50-110, while they have undoubted merit, will probably soon give way to cartridges of like caliber and greater power. For instance, the .50-110, and the Winchester .405 have practically the same ballistics, like weight of bullet, velocity, and striking force, yet few would select the .50 in preference to the .405. However, should the .50 be remodeled to take a 400 grain bullet with a powder charge that would drive it 2,500 feet a second it would find admirers, notwithstanding the fact that for American use it would have a surplus of power.

Fashions change in rifles and cartridges almost

as readily as with ladies' hats. The present tendency is to discard good and well tried ammunition of moderate ballistics in favor of larger bores of extreme power, and military ammunition of velocity approaching 3,000 feet; this will shortly be made the military standard velocity it seems, and many game shooters will also prefer it.

The latest hobby among big game hunters is a sharp-pointed (or Spitzer) full mantled bullet-- this for large or even dangerous game. The claim is made for such missiles that they must replace the soft-nose, because the latter is not accurate when driven at a velocity of 3,000 feet, and that the soft ball must have considerably increased weight or it will mushroom and not penetrate. All of this may be quite true, but since a great deal of experimenting is still going on, perhaps it would be wise to render the Scotch verdict of " not proven."

For convenience I have classified cartridges as: miniature and gallery, small game, match rifle, military and sporting, number 1, military and sporting, number 2, and large-bore, high power. Subsequently every cartridge that I deem worthy of it will be given individual mention and its proper uses outlined.

RIFLE CARTRIDGES

Under the head of miniature will be included cartridges that are actually too small for anything that could really be considered game for the rifle. The .22 short is typical of this class. All of this ammunition is rimfire.

Small game cartridges are all center fire, are for the most part loaded with smokeless powder, have from fair to high velocities, and vary in power from rabbit loads to deer. The special uses of the different calibers and cartridges will be noted.

Match rifle cartridges are limited in number, embracing only those that have been found to give the finest results in off-hand shooting at two hundred yards. Formerly match cartridges might have included those adapted to work up to a thousand yards, but of late years long range match shooting is entirely military, not coming under the head of the match rifle.

Military and sporting, number 1, includes such ammunition as has heretofore been popular with hunters, of which the Remington .35 and the Winchester .33 are typical. All of those in this list are of moderate ballistics, accurate and reliable, and of low breech pressure.

Cartridges, military and sporting, number 2, comprise those of the latest design and the most pronounced ballistics. The general characteristics of the class are light, sharp-pointed bullets, heavy powder charges relative to the lead, and very high velocities.

Of the large bore, high-power, we have but a limited number of cartridges for which our rifles are chambered, but nearly all weapons designed for African use come under this heading. The Winchester .405 is an American example of the high-power, big-bore. In the next chapter we will take up the various classes at length.

CHAPTER VIII

MINIATURE AND GALLERY—SMALL GAME

.22 Short. .22 Long rifle. .22 Winchester R.
F. .22 Automatic. .25 Stevens.

THESE cartridges have the same general
characteristics, light bullets, low velocity,
slight report, and a trifling amount of
power. Usually one and all of them are cata·
loged as the proper thing for small game. It depends greatly upon the definition of small game;
if we mean song and insectivorous birds the
catalogs are right. If, however, small game
means turkey, geese, coyotes, woodchucks, foxes,
or jack-rabbits, not one of the above cartridges
is worth considering. Of course, they will kill
sometimes, kill a steer if the bullet is placed in
the brain, but following the principle of big game
hunters who require a rifle that will kill instantly
where the ball strikes fairly, all the .22 rimfires
will be found inadequate.

The amount of cruelty and mischief compassed by the .22 rimfires would be startling if known in its entirety. Recently, near my home, where I had been carefully protecting the song birds, I had the pleasure of watching a man out for his daily practice with a .22 automatic. He killed one bluejay that flew fifty yards before falling, dying after its head had been pounded. Of three doves shot at, one got away feathered; one flew some distance, tried to alight on a tree, fell off, and was shot again; a third fell dead after making quite a flight. A mocking bird had one leg shot off, and I have seen it a number of times since, hopping about on its remaining leg. One blue bird and three other little fellows were killed dead on the spot.

The .22 rimfire is the favorite rifle of boys and a certain lawless class of our resident alien population, before whom everything that gets up in front of the gun is game, song birds preferred. The average so-called small game shooter starts out for an afternoon's sport with about two hundred cartridges, and if there is any wild thing which does not draw a shot, the hunter is not the average I am speaking of but an exception. I should estimate that half the little birds that were once in America have been killed by the .22 short and the single barrel shotgun. If the Audubon Society has the real interest of our songsters at heart it will fire a broadside at these misnamed small game rifles in place of the automatic shotgun.

The real province of the .22's is gallery and short range target work. With them a foundation can be laid for rifle shooting skill, and later an arm can be taken up with which something can be killed in a sportsmanlike manner.

The .22 caliber R. F. is the rifle for the beginner. It cannot be used at long range so none of the problems which later puzzle the rifleman, such as light, wind, atmosphere, temperature, humidity, or elevation are connected with its use. The task of the miniature rifleman is simply one of holding, aiming, and pulling trigger, and he who fails to perfect himself in these has but himself to blame.

THE .22 SHORT

This cartridge contains three grains of powder and thirty of lead, and can be had either in black or smokeless powder. As noted under the general heading, it has been extensively advertised as the correct thing for small game shooting, but neither the .22 short, .22 long-rifle, nor .22 automatic has the range, trajectory, or power that a game rifle should possess.

In the gallery, however, the .22 short has a special field of its own. The very highest possible scores have been made with it, and it is the consensus of opinion among expert riflemen that the .22 short is as accurate as any cartridge made up to seventy-five feet, when used indoors. The points of this cartridge which appeal to the gallery shot are, accuracy, cheapness, cleanliness, light report, and little smoke, all important requisites in the gallery. The outdoor snapshot prefers the cartridge for similar reasons, though accuracy is of less importance to him. If the .22 short is to be used on game, head shots alone should be taken.

THE .22 LONG RIFLE

This cartridge is loaded with five grains of powder and forty of lead, and the powder may be either black or smokeless, the former giving a trifle the higher velocity.

The long-rifle takes the place of the .22 short when it comes to outdoor target practice, since the heavier bullet is much less sensitive to wind. Up to a hundred yards it will do good work in any ordinary weather and will make a close pattern at two hundred yards on a still day. However, a moderate wind will drift the bullet two feet at the latter range, and therefore its use is not practical beyond one hundred yards. Of all the ammunition made this one seems to be able to fire the largest number of shots without loss of accuracy from fouling, which makes it a prime favorite with short range target shots.

As a game cartridge it will do for squirrels and rabbits but the hollow point bullet should be used or many animals will escape wounded. Its trajectory is too high for it to be used with much success at ranges beyond fifty yards—this for unknown and estimated distances.

THE .22 AUTOMATIC

The .22 automatic is very similar in ballistic properties to the long-rifle, when the latter is loaded with smokeless powder. It uses a forty-five grain hardened bullet which promotes penetration without adding to killing power. Like the foregoing it is a splendid cartridge for continuous, non-fouling target practice, being a great favorite with professional fancy rifle shots, owing to the weapon in which it is used, its cleanliness, freedom from recoil, and accuracy.

THE .22 WINCHESTER RIMFIRE

For various reasons this is a better hunting cartridge than either of those mentioned above. It has more power, driving a forty-five grain bullet with seven grains of powder. The bullet is seated in the shell with no lubricant exposed, wherein it has the advantage of the .22 short or the long-rifle, neither of which can be carried loose in the pocket. Moreover, it is a better cartridge for a repeating rifle since the ball is crimped to the shell and will not jerk out letting powder spill into the action. If sport can be had shooting such birds as quail, doves, and snipe, with a rifle, this cartridge would prove effective. Both pump and single-shot rifles are chambered for it in addition to the Colt revolver.

THE .25-11-65 STEVENS RIMFIRE

Limiting small game to birds of a size less than turkey, and not considering trajectory as a factor in landing our bullet on the mark, this cartridge will do the work. It kills squirrels and rabbits very cleanly when struck in the fore part of the body. For a combination of killing qualities on birds without undue smashing it has few rivals. Its power can be considered as roughly double that of any of the .22 rimfires. The rifleman who uses it upon game at ranges beyond sixty yards must be an expert judge of distances.

The .25 Stevens rimfire has accomplished very fine work at two hundred yards off-hand. While the .25-11 is a splendid short range target cartridge, superior even to the long-rifle, yet its use has been restricted by the increased cost as compared with the .22 rimfires.

SMALL GAME RIFLES—TARGET RIFLES FOR SHORT UNKNOWN DISTANCES

The demands upon a rifle intended for woodchuck, geese, turkey, coyotes, foxes, hawks, crows, jackrabbits, cottontails, and squirrels, are that it must have ample power, the trajectory must be flat enough to shoot at any distance up to one hundred yards without change of sight, the arm itself should be light, the accuracy must be good for a long series of shots, and the ammunition inexpensive. Not all of the cartridges mentioned comply with the condition fully, and some are better adapted to one species of game than another—as will be shown. Perhaps we should have limited this small game ammunition to nitro powder shells, but a couple of those listed, while loaded with black powder, have enough merit to be included.

Preferably ammunition for this sort of shooting should have a minimum velocity of not less than 1,800 feet, with a muzzle energy of at least 500 pounds, but we have only a few cartridges that will meet these requirements, and must, therefore, accept others. For game like rabbits and squirrels a lower velocity and less energy are all right, but for shooting above one hundred yards flat trajectory is very important.

It should be borne in mind that rifles of the class we are treating here are intended as much as anything for rifle training, shooting in the woods and fields at various marks, unknown distances up to three hundred yards. Bullets for this purpose must have range, accuracy, flat trajectory, and not be too much affected by the wind. Moreover, the question of recoil is not to be overlooked where the novice is being put through his paces—a kicking rifle would have to go into some other class.

.22-13-45 WINCHESTER AND .22-15-60 STEVENS

For the sake of economy in space we will bracket these two cartridges together. The former has a trifle more velocity and the latter somewhat greater power. The trajectory of either is about two and a half inches at one hundred yards, the velocity a trifle better than 1,500 feet, the energy 237 to 275 foot pounds.

As target cartridges neither would compare with some of the rimfire .22's, since the heavy black powder charge fouls too much, but as game cartridges they are superior. Either of them is capable of keeping ten shots in a four-inch circle at one hundred yards. Both of them could be improved by being charged with smokeless powder behind a metal patched bullet, and perhaps this will be done some time. Loaded with nitro powder, giving a muzzle velocity of 2,000 feet, they would have a much wider field of usefulness. At present they are chiefly useful for work on rabbits, squirrels, hawks, and crows, though with hollow-point bullets they will kill larger game. Only single shot rifles are chambered for these two cartridges.

THE .25-20-86 STEVENS AND .25-20 MARLIN AND WINCHESTER

Here we have cartridges that, while not of the same shape and not interchangeable, have practically the same ballistics—when loaded with black powder. The former can be used only in single-shot rifles and the latter only in repeaters. The .25-20 repeater cartridge loaded with black powder gives the ordinary 1,400 feet velocity and with smokeless increases the velocity to 1,700 feet.

This feature of the cartridge makes it perhaps the best now obtainable as combined small game and general practice ammunition. The shell takes a greater variety of charges, designed for more special uses than any other I know. It can be charged with ten grains of black, semi-smokeless, or an equivalent amount of smokeless powder and a seventy-seven grain, sharp pointed bullet wherewith even small birds like quail may be shot through the body without mutilation. Then the regular black powder cartridge is an especially good one up to two hundred yards, splendid scores having been made with it on the Standard American and German Ring targets at the distance. The .25-20 is also a great promotor of economical rifle practice since it lends itself admirably to hand reloaded ammunition. The rifle lover can mold his bullets to different tempers and shapes, and make up his ammunition entire if he likes, or lubricated factory bullets can be bought at a trifling cost, and half the price of ammunition saved.

The regular black powder charge has a muzzle energy of 360 foot pounds, a trajectory of 2.88 inches, an accuracy of a three-inch circle at one hundred yards. This black cartridge is quite capable of accounting for any of the birds or animals mentioned at the beginning of this chapter, when fired upon at ranges not exceeding a hundred and fifty yards. If the rifleman has occasion to shoot beyond this distance the high velocity, smokeless ammunition will be found suited to his purpose.

The .25-20 high velocity has an initial speed of 1,712 feet, one hundred yard trajectory 1.85 inches, energy 560 pounds. There is no question of its effectiveness on anything smaller than deer, and even those animals would be stopped if struck right. The high velocity charge increases the practical killing range of the .25-20 from a hundred and fifty to two hundred yards.

There are two other black powder cartridges that have about the same ballistics as the .25-20. These are the .25-21 and the .25-25 Stevens. The shells of these are straight inside, a feature that renders them easy to reload and keep clean, and they are well liked by the experimental rifleman.

RIFLES AND RIFLE SHOOTING

THE .22 NEWTON-SAVAGE HIGH-POWER

This cartridge is the latest development of ammunition and rifle for small game shooting. The powder charge is twenty-five grains of Du-Pont Lightning, and the metal patched, sharp-pointed, soft-nose bullet weighs seventy grains. It is given an initial velocity of 2,761 feet, and its trajectory up to two hundred yards is practically the same as that of the '06 Springfield. The accurate range of this ammunition is over five hundred yards, but it is not intended for a long range rifle, but for work on small game and for that attractive outdoor rifle practice of which marksmen are so fond.

There is no doubt but this cartridge will prove effective on anything up to deer, having about the same power as the .25-35. For shooting at estimated distances up to say three hundred yards I believe it to be the best cartridge that we have, since it comes as near to shooting point blank at two hundred yards as anything now built in this country. The moderate recoil of this cartridge and gun would further accuracy when used by the average rifleman who has not been trained with military arms.

For work on such beasts as coyote, woodchuck, or fox the soft-nose bullet could be used with paralyzing effect. Where smashing was not desired, a full mantled ball would be best. The shell can also be reloaded with a fifty grain bullet, and a reduced powder charge for lesser game like squirrels and rabbits. The twist of the rifling, one turn in twelve inches, is such that plain lead bullets and reduced powder charges will work nicely.

On the whole it appears that the Newton-Savage is the last word in small game rifles. It is not intended for shooting tiny birds, but neither are they "small game." This cartridge is adapted to the lever-action repeater made by the Savage Arms Company.

CHAPTER IX

MATCH RIFLE CARTRIDGES AND THEIR MANIPULA-
TION—28-30-120,-32-40, .33 POPE

MATCH rifle shooting or Schuetzen work
has now come to mean off-hand shooting at two hundred yards exclusively.
For this purpose the choice of cartridges has
narrowed down to those listed above. The re-
quisite qualities of such ammunition are: the
greatest possible accuracy, weight enough of
bullet to be steady in the wind, and a practical
absence of recoil. A balance of accuracy, steadiness, and freedom from recoil are insisted upon
by the Schuetzen man, and one quality would not
be tolerated if gained at the expense of another.
As an example the .38-55 once in general use, is
no longer in great favor, because what this larger
bore gained in steadiness it lost through its
"kick" with the resulting undue strain under
which the marksman labored. On the other
hand while the .25 caliber is very accurate and

76

without recoil, it is too sensitive to wind for any but good weather conditions.

As a result the choice of match rifle cartridges has almost narrowed to the .28-50, .32-40, and .33. Again the preference for one of these would be governed by the constitutional tendencies of the rifleman. If he has a delicately adjusted nervous organization the chances are he is partial to the .28, while a more rugged man would do his best work with the .33, because less annoyed by changes in the wind.

It is not to be disputed that the match rifle and its cartridges are the most accurate combination ever made for work at two hundred yards, and to me it seems doubtful if the present output can be improved upon in the future. The cartridges alone cannot be credited entirely with this hair-splitting accuracy, neither can the rifles from which they are shot, for much of it is due to carefully considered manipulation of rifle and ammunition.

From the beginning the match rifleman has utterly condemned the ordinary fixed ammunition such as is used in hunting rifles. Usually he has a preference for heavier bullets than the standard, the very heaviest bullets that his rifle will spin without tipping, finding that these will group closer. Some have been content to load these heavy bullets in the mouth of the shell with nearly all grooves exposed, so that closing the action forced the ball up into the rifling. Others considered this but a half measure and by the use of a bullet seater, placed the ball quite ahead of the shell. The intent in either case was the same, to get the bullet seated in the center of the bore so that it could not start in a tipping manner or "shave" lead as it took the rifling.

In former days a great problem was to maintain a uniform cleanness of bore, with an entire absence of leading. I might state here, parenthetically, that I have never yet seen a rifle with lead bullets crimped into the shell that would fire a hundred shots without showing traces of lead in the bore, or that would maintain accuracy for this number of rounds. Sometimes the elevation will change as the lead deposits, in other instances a wild shot will be thrown now and then; the worse the leading the poorer the results. A rifle that would stay in a six-inch circle with the first score might be scattering all over a twenty-four inch before the hundred was finished.

Knowing this, many careful marksmen preferred patched bullets, seated ahead of the shell, the rifle being invariably cleaned between rounds.

So manipulated, the rifle gained greatly in regular accuracy, and nearly all the finest scores of a decade or two ago were made with this style of loading. I need not go into it further here because the patch bullet is now nearly obsolete.

Finally the Pope System of rifle boring and loading solved all the problems of the Schuetzen man, leaving him nothing to do but to load his weapon and shoot. The Pope-Stevens rifle is cut with narrow lands and a gain twist, starting slow at the breech and reaching the desired turn at the muzzle. It has a false muzzle, starter, and ramrod, through the use of which the bullet is started at the muzzle and pushed down to the breech where it rests just in front of the shell chamber. Then the shell is filled with powder and, without a wad, is placed in behind the ball the same as in any other breechloader. The bullet has a very square base, and a broad band at the bottom; as it goes down it pushes the fouling before it, leaving the barrel uniformly clean. The barrel is slightly choked at the muzzle and the lands are narrow and so shaped as to cause little friction; as a consequence after the ball passes through the false muzzle it seats very easily, perfectly centered in the bore.

These rifles can be shot all day without any

attention being paid to the bore and at night will be as accurate as when work was begun in the morning. Further, they are the most accurate rifles made anywhere of any description. With one of them ten shots have been placed in an inch and a half circle at two hundred yards when shot with a machine rest, and fifty shots in a three-inch.

I should regard the accuracy of rifles, all equally well cut but with different styles of loading, as something like this: A .32-40 rifle with fixed ammunition will shoot ten shots into a six-inch circle but the accuracy will go off before fifty shots are fired. With heavy bullets loaded uncrimped in the muzzle of the shell, ten shots can be placed in a five-inch and fifty in an eight. Where the bullets are seated ahead of the shell from the breech with a bullet seater, ten shots might be kept in a four-inch circle and fifty in a six-inch. Patched bullets will pattern still closer. With the average Pope rifle and its accessories ten shots should be kept in a two-inch and fifty in a three-inch at the distance. Any of this work implies that weather conditions shall be favorable with little wind to affect the bullet's flight.

Black powder and King's semi-smokeless are

the favorite compounds with sharpshooters. Whichever propellant may be selected, it is customary to prime it with a few grains of nitro powder which assist in blowing out the dirt and keeping the bore clean. Flasks are made especially to prime shells with the smokeless and follow with the black with almost one motion, the whole loading being more uniformly accomplished than could be done by dipping.

Pope-Stevens rifles always take heavier bullets than the standard. The .25 caliber 86 grain bullet is replaced by one of 98 grains; the .28-120 grain by one of 140 grains; the .32 uses a 200 grain ball, .33, 220 and .38, 300 grain. All of these bullets have blunt points with a long bearing in the rifling. The shells, of course, being filled to the top, hold more than the normal charge of powder, the .25-25 shell will hold nearly 30 grains and so on with the others.

Which of these calibers to select is something for the individual rifleman to settle for himself. If he has any inclination to flinch, the chances are he does his best work with a .25. The average gallery, trained sharpshooter will likely secure the best results from the .28, while the veteran on the range will cling to his .30-40 or .33. The .38-55 will tire out any but the most rugged marksman ere a day's work is finished. It should always be kept in mind that a man may fire two hundred shots or more in the course of a day.

CHAPTER X

Rifles for Deer, Antelope, Caribou, Black Bear, Mountain Lions. Calibers—.25-35-117 Winchester, .25-35 Remington Automatic, .32-40 High Power, .30-30 Winchester and Marlin, .303 Savage, .32 Special, .30 Remington Automatic, .33 Winchester, .35 Remington, and .35 Winchester.

I HAVE seen fit to separate our hunting cartridges into classes 1 and 2, partly on the ground that one class was designed exclusively for hunting purposes and the other as a rule for military use, partly for the reason that they differ essentially in ballistics.

Those listed in class 1 are strictly game cartridges, no army rifles ever having been chambered for anyone of them. On the contrary those embraced in class 2 were either originally intended for military arms or they have been modeled after the military ammunition. A radical difference in the two classes of cartridges is that those of class 1 are rarely used with other than soft-nose bullets, while expert opinion leans to the belief that the number 2 class are more effective with full mantled, sharp pointed bullets.

The cartridges heading this chapter, though varying widely in caliber and energy, yet otherwise have very similar ballistics. They unite in a happy medium of range, power, accuracy, velocity, trajectory, and moderate recoil. Undoubtedly some of them would be found much better adapted to certain purposes than others, yet all have been thoroughly tested by American big game hunters and have proved to fulfill admirably the purpose for which they were designed.

Excluding the .25 calibers, many consider that any of the cartridges in this class have all the power needed for any game on the American Continent. Free recoil is something to be considered in the choice of a rifle, and with the exception of the .350 Winchester all of those listed in class 1 are of the non-kicking persuasion. Moreover breech pressures are light compared with those in class 2, and this furthers length of life in a barrel with absence of metallic fouling and other troubles most familiar to the military man. Practically all of them use soft-nose bullets exclusively, handling them with regular accuracy. Velocities in these cartridges vary from 1,985 feet for the Savage to 2,200 for the Winchester .35.

I will now briefly outline the special points of the different cartridges in class 1.

.25-35 WINCHESTER AND .25-35 REMINGTON AUTOMATIC

Ballistically these cartridges might be considered as one, though the Remington has over a hundred feet the higher velocity and the shell is different, being rimless.

Many species of game, including elk and bear, have been killed with the .25-35, but I think it would be wise to restrict their big game use to deer. They have a muzzle energy of from 1,000 to 1,200 foot pounds, but this falls short of the 1,500 pounds that might be considered the minimum for big game shooting of a general description.

The slight recoil of the little cartridges, only three and a third pounds, renders them especially attractive for general rifle practice, including target practice up to five hundred yards, training in the woods and fields with a view to promoting the correct judging of distance, and for that quick and accurate snap work for which the rifleman of the future will be noted. For shooting all small game of the "varmint" variety this is a splendid cartridge.

By reason of its being made of a more modern type, rimless, because of its higher velocity, and because it is used by an automatic rifle, the Remington cartridge will probably outlive the other. The Winchester cartridge is furnished in reduced charges for such game as squirrels and rabbits, thus making it a fairly good all-round rifle for certain sections of the country.

THE .30-30, .32-40, .32 SPECIAL, .303 SAVAGE, .30 REMINGTON AUTOMATIC

These cartridges are so similar in all essential properties that if all but one were done away with the others would hardly be missed. The Savage has a heavier bullet than any of the others with the consequent greater penetration, but its velocity is also somewhat lower which makes its energy about the same. The .32 Special has the highest velocity and greatest smashing force, but not to any marked extent. The .32-40 with its straight tapered shell and slower twist of rifling lends itself to a variety of loads, including black powder charges, and many believe that, taken all round, it is the best of the lot. Striking force in this lot of cartridges varies only from 1,540 to 1,684 pounds.

Cartridges of the .30-30 type can be considered the most conservative and most fully tested of any used in American hunting rifles. Perhaps the .30-30 has killed more big game in the last ten years than any other cartridge in use. We know what this ammunition will do because it has done it again and again.

It has always impressed me that for use in the Northern or Eastern woods, on any game less than grizzly bear, the sportsman would be perfectly safe in selecting any one of the above cartridges, confident that he had made a wise choice of the cartridge and the hunting arm which handles it. These cartridges are all shot from lever-action rifles except the Remington Auto.

THE .33 WINCHESTER, .35 REMINGTON, .401 WINCHESTER

To all intents and purposes, so far as results upon game are concerned, these three cartridges may be considered as one and the same. All of them use 200 grain bullets, and while the Winchester .401 has some little advantage in velocity, trajectory, and energy, the difference is not of sufficient moment to be worthy of special mention. All have muzzle velocities of 2,000 feet and better, with a striking force in the neighborhood of a ton. The character and shape of the soft-point bullet used is the same in all.

While I believe that in view of present tendencies and preferences among riflemen and game hunters this ammunition could be improved by increasing the velocity to 2,400 or 2,500 feet, yet I consider them at the present time, for general use, the best all round big game cartridges we have in America. They have such diameter and shape of bullet as will insure against upset and the expenditure of the full energy upon any game, whether soft skinned or heavy boned. Moreover, power, accuracy, and trajectory are accompanied in them by low breech pressure, little metallic fouling or wear on the barrels, and a minimum of recoil for results secured.

In the hands of experienced guides, mountain men, and hunters in the West and North these cartridges and the guns in which they are used have given perfect results upon all game including the largest varieties of bear. This is not saying that they are bear or elephant guns, but they will do the work when required, and certainly have ample power for elk and moose.

THE .35 WINCHESTER

This cartridge might fairly have been placed with the big bores, but falls short of the 3,000 pounds of muzzle energy that is the minimum with them, so I have put it in the present class. In power it shows what the .33 Winchester and .35 Remington might have accomplished if given a few hundred feet greater velocity. The .35 Winchester is well liked by all those who have a partiality for ample power and do not mind the recoil which must accompany it. In all respects, striking force, velocity, and trajectory, it is an advance upon the preceding cartridges, having an energy at one hundred yards equalling the others at the muzzle.

There are many other cartridges, like the .30-40-220 Krag, .303 British, 7, 8, and 9 mm. Mauser which might have been placed in class 1, but they are being remodeled to take heavier powder charges in connection with light Spitzer bullets and so have been promoted to class 2,

RIFLES AND RIFLE SHOOTING

Rifles adapted to shooting Moose, Elk, Grizzly
Bear, Mountain Sheep, Goats, and all Amer-
ican game. Calibers—.236 Lee-Navy, .256
Mannlicher, .25-50-117 Newton High-Power, 7,
and 8 mm. Mauser-Spitzer, .280 Ross, 30-'06
Springfield, .275-303 Axite.

As previously stated, cartridges embraced in
this class were either originally designed for long
range military use, or they have been modeled
after this type of ammunition. With the exception of the .275-300 Axite, all the above are alike
in every essential ballistic quality. Those of
most recent design are the highest in velocity,
which aptly illustrates the tendencies of the
times. Velocities range from 2,500 feet for the
Mannlicher to 3,500 feet for the Newton High-
Power.

With the one exception noted, considered as
game cartridges, they are an absolute departure
from accepted conclusions. Previous to their
invention it was not doubted that soft-point bullets were more effective on game than full metal
patched, or that blunt points had a smashing
effect that the sharp lacked. Now we are con-

fronted with the theory, not unsupported by proof, that the sharp-point, full mantle is the most deadly form of projectile when driven at a velocity approaching 8,000 feet. Accepting the theory as true, we can only account for it by acknowledging as a fact the statement that given speed enough a bullet will upset anyhow, no matter what its shape or metal covering.

Further the speedy ball must have an explosive effect on animal tissue not unlike its manner of bursting a can of tomatoes. So pronounced is this explosive quality in the highly driven bullet that I am told the tiny .22 Newton-Savage is more deadly on deer than the .30-30. Whatever the reason that may be assigned, such rifle experts as Lieut. Whelen, Roosevelt, White, Crossman, and others pronounce the '06 Springfield the most deadly form of 150 grain missile that ever struck animal flesh.

Whether time and further experience will modify the views of these experts or not, and I believe they will be modified, the whole tendency of cartridge designers of the immediate future will be in the direction of still further increasing bullet velocity, thereby promoting that peculiarly deadly effect mentioned.

It seems probable that while raising the

velocity with improved and stronger powders, the bullets will be lengthened from the present short and light missiles, thus furthering accuracy and speed of flight at long range. Taking the '06 Springfield as the type, and all the others are modeled after it, the ball loses velocity too rapidly after traveling five hundred yards to be acceptable as the military bullet of the future. The 2,700 feet initial velocity of the Springfield has fallen to 1,068 feet at one thousand yards, a loss of 1,632 feet over the range. In view of the fact that long range military shooting will finally be lengthened to two thousand yards, this falling off in velocity is altogether too rapid.

We are not treating military arms or military shooting, but the desirability of maintaining velocity in game work is this: Unless there is a miracle in the little sharp pointed ball, its effectiveness is entirely due to its velocity. When its speed drops to 1,200 feet it will have no more effect on the animal struck than any other ball of like size and shape traveling at the given rate. If it takes 2,500 feet of velocity to " explode " animal tissue, we must maintain this speed up to the point where the bullet lands in the game. This the Springfield 150 grain will not do if it is to be used at ranges from two to three hundred yards greater than our ordinary game rifles, as our experts declare that it can be.

I think that we, the conservative and the radical alike, can make up our minds that the day of the 3,000 foot velocity hunting cartridge is upon us. The known and the good will have to give way, first to the experimental, and then to the perfected cartridge of the future. Class 1, ammunition will at last yield to class 2, though these may be modified considerably from those that at present hold sway.

Game of the future is going to be scarcer and wilder, necessitating shots at longer distances. Trajectory must then be considered of the utmost importance. Moreover the rifleman of the next decade will be better trained to snap and running shots than any marksmen we now have, and whether the bullet lands in a quarter of a second or a half second will make a wonderful difference, where the target is two or three hundred yards away and traveling at the rate of thirty or forty feet a second.

To the credit of the new type of ammunition, too, it should be remembered that it is the most accurate sporting ammunition in use. Experiments by the War Department demonstrate that the '06 ammunition will keep ten shots in a three-inch circle at two hundred yards while the soft-point bullet of the .30-40 and similar rifles will only pattern in an eight-inch. Granted that game is to be killed at three hundred yards and farther, we must have the accurate cartridge.

With the exception of the .275-303 which has been included in class 2 because of its high velocity and small bore, all the cartridges in this class are as like as the peas in a pod. Some of them may be loaded with different sizes of ball, but the characteristics and the ballistic data given have reference only to the Spitzer bullet.

The 6 mm. or .236 U. S. Navy has never been extensively used in sport, but this was not from lack of merit, but because the rifle from which it was shot was neither well known nor easily obtained. The rifle for this cartridge is no longer made, yet at this time there is a tendency to extol the merits of both rifle and cartridge. The 112 grain bullet has an initial velocity of 2,562 feet, energy 1,632 foot pounds, 200 yard trajectory 3.49 inches.

The .256 Mannlicher is very like the .236 Navy, except that its bullet is heavier and its striking force something greater. It has been used extensively abroad but not very much in this country. Almost every species of big game has been killed with the .256 Mannlicher, even to elephants, and at one time it was the fashion to pronounce it more deadly than the big bores. A more extensive use showed this conclusion wrong, but it seems to have execution sufficient for any of the deer family.

The latest candidate for the favor of the high velocity, Spitzer bullet devotee is the .25-50-117 Newton Savage High-Power. The cartridge has not been used enough to afford any very reliable data as to what it will do, especially on game. However, there is no reason to doubt but that it will be as successful as others of its class. Its bullets shows the highest experimental velocity of any cartridge ever built, 3,500 feet, and its striking energy is about the same as that of the Springfield '06.

The characteristics and ballistics of the New Springfield have been treated in the preceding pages. It has been pronounced the most accurate military cartridge made, a claim our Canadian neighbors are disposed to dispute with the .280 Ross.

The Springfield has made many possibles at all ranges in the hands of our troops and won the international matches, while the Ross last year carried off the highest honors in England.

The Ross .280 has a velocity some four hundred feet higher than that of the Springfield, a bullet of the same shape but weighing a few grains less, and the claim is made for it that it has less chamber pressure than the '06. The accuracy of the Ross is said to equal that of the Springfield.

The 7 mm and the 8 mm Mauser-Spitzer are designed exactly like the Ross and the Springfield. There is hardly a doubt but they will have the same capabilities. Their initial velocities are a trifle short of 3,000 feet. Full ballistics of these cartridges will be found in the table.

The .375-303 Axite is a development of the .303 British Army cartridge. It is loaded with the same weight and shape of bullet, 215 grains, but the powder charge has been increased to give a muzzle velocity of from 2,500 to 2,600 feet. The muzzle energy is about 3,000 pounds, and this with soft-point ball makes its power ample for ordinary large game.

CHAPTER XI

BIG BORE, HIGH POWER CARTRIDGES

Rifles for Grizzly Bear and Big Game of Asia and Africa. Lions, Tigers, Rhino, Hippo,— Elephant Guns. Calibers.—.405 Winchester, .318 Westley Richards. .333 Jeffery, .400, .404, .450, .475, .500, .577, .600.

MOST of the cartridges that are included in this class are built in Europe. They are of such variety and numbers as to preclude mention of more than a few, and those of a sort that American sportsmen might have occasion to use. I have seen fit to set the minimum caliber of this class at .218 and the striking force demanded at not less than 3,000 foot pounds. This is the minimum; nearly all the cartridges are larger, up to the .600 with a muzzle energy of over 8,000 pounds.

From the best information obtainable it seems that an African sportsman would consider an energy of from 3,000 to 4,000 pounds about the right thing for the larger African antelope, lions, and tigers. A striking force of from 4,000 to 5,000 pounds would do for rhino, hippo, and buffalo. Above 5,000 the weapon might be considered as purely an elephant gun.

It might be noted here that our own .405 Winchester is the baby of the lot, though it has been used very effectively on lions, leopards, rhinos, hippos, buffalo, and all game smaller than elephants by Roosevelt, White, and other Americans. In this country we are in the habit of considering the .405 a sort of hand cannon, but it is all a matter of comparison. The .600 Jeffrey strikes at one hundred yards with three times the force of the .405.

THE .405 WINCHESTER

This is the most powerful cartridge adapted to the lever action rifle, or in fact any American rifle except a few handmade arms.

Besides the work accomplished with **it in** Africa as mentioned, it is well liked by hunters who have made trips to Alaska and the Northwest for the giant brown bear, moose, and like game.

Whether it is powerful enough for African

buffalo and rhinoceros is a debatable question, most people would decide not, and Roosevelt did a lot of hitting for one kill sometimes, but there is no disputing that it has all the knock-down qualities needed for the most rugged game in this country. The .405 is too destructive for deer, antelope, and animals of that size; neither can many men shoot such ammunition with the same accuracy that they could lighter charges. The man who is recoil proof and desirous of killing cleanly with one bullet should take very kindly to the .405.

One advantage of this cartridge should not be overlooked when comparing it with other big bores. It is shot from the fastest action of any ammunition at all approaching it in strength, and this must be given due weight where it might be necessary to give a dangerous animal more than one bullet. American hunters in Africa have always felt pretty safe with the .405 Winchester in their hands, whatever the beast they might be facing.

The .405 has a muzzle velocity of 2,204 feet, muzzle energy 3,206 foot pounds, 200 yard trajectory 4.85 inches, and the arm from which it is shot is model '95 Winchester, weighing eight and a half pounds.

RIFLES AND RIFLE SHOOTING

These two cartridges belong to the most advanced type of big bore, high velocity, hunting ammunition. The .318 drives a 250 grain ball with a muzzle velocity of 2,500 feet; the .333 has the same weight of bullet which it sends at the rate of 2,600 feet. Both of the cartridges are loaded with projectiles of various kinds, weights, and shapes, full-mantled, sharp-pointed, soft-nosed, hollow pointed, and copper capped.

With the sharp-point, full mantled ball the Jeffery is said to have the greatest penetration of any hunting bullet made—sufficient to shoot clean through an elephant. Also it is one of the flattest shooting of rifles at long range, maintaining its velocity better than the lighter bullets of military design. The .318 is charged with Axite powder, the .333 with cordite, and both are declared to be extremely accurate at any and all ranges, even exceeding a thousand yards.

From reports of hunters in Asia and Africa the .318 and .333 will give a good account of themselves upon any game that lives. However, their especial field is long range shots in the open at game that requires hard hitting and yet is not particularly dangerous. Most Englishmen have a penchant for still more powerful ammunition where animals have to be shot in cover and stopped instantly, like a tiger for instance.

The ballistics of the .318 are, velocity 2,400 to 2,500 feet, energy at muzzle 3,400 pounds, breech pressure 19 tons, 200 yard trajectory 4 inches, weight of ball 250 grains. The .333 has an initial velocity of 2,600 feet, striking force 4,000 pounds, 200 yard trajectory 3 inches, length of bullet 1½ inches, breech pressure 20 tons, shell contains a large air space, free recoil 35 pounds. Like the foregoing this cartridge is shot from double rifles, single-shots, and bolt-actions. Guns for the .318 are made by Westley Richards, the .333 by Jeffery.

.400, .404, .450, .475, .500.   JUNGLE RIFLES

There is a good deal of similarity in ballistics of the above cartridges, and I have not space to go into them in detail. Their velocities are all in the neighborhood of 2,200 feet, the bullets weigh from 400 to 570 grains, and the muzzle energies are from 4,000 to 5,200 pounds.

All are designed for the very largest game and especially for use in the jungle where a dangerous beast must be stopped in its tracks with a single bullet. Greener asserts that the .500 bore is the largest that should ever have been built in a cordite rifle, those larger having an unbearable recoil. It is impossible to obtain exact figures for the free recoil of the above cartridges, but I should estimate it at from 45 to 60 pounds. I notice our African game shooters are chary about shooting one of these weapons except when the case looks grave. In any event I doubt if anything heavier than the .475-80-500 Jeffery with a striking force of 5,000 pounds, is necessary to kill a whale.

One thing might be noted about these powerful cordite cartridges: All of them are loaded with an amount of powder which permits a considerable air space in the shell, in some instances the shell would hold nearly double the amount of powder placed in it. The purpose of this air space is to reduce breech pressure, which it is said to do very effectively.

Here is a statement from Jeffery in regard to this: "The Jeffery .400 case holds, when filled to the top of the case, 120 grains of water, and the 60 grains of cordite fill the space of 40 grains of water, cordite being practically one-third heavier than water." We thus see that in this shell the powder charge takes up but one-third of the space. Mr. Jeffery gives the breech pressure of one of these giant cartridges as from 14 to 15 tons, something less than half that of the tiny .226—112 U. S. Navy, as originally built.

577 CORDITE, 600 CORDITE.   ELEPHANT GUNS

Formerly big game hunters, like Sir Samuel Baker and others, used eight and four bores for elephant shooting, loaded with from fourteen to sixteen drams of black powder and a spherical ball or a cylindrical bullet with hardened point. These huge arms have gradually gone out of use. being replaced by the .577 and .600 cordite rifles.

The .577 drives a bullet of 750 grains with a velocity of 2,050 feet and possesses a striking force of 5,680 foot pounds. The .600 Jeffery is the most powerful rifle made, not excepting the four bore. Its bullet weighs 900 grains, powder charge 100 grains cordite, velocity 2,000 feet. Both the striking force and the velocity vary somewhat with climate, being 2,000 feet and 8,000 pounds in England, compared with 2,100 feet and 8,700 pounds in India.

Mr. Jeffery naively states that owing to the recoil this rifle cannot be shot accurately at long range. I should roughly estimate the recoil at a hundred pounds and a man standing near it when it is fired should place pads in his ears and stand on his toes. I can safely recommend the arm to the hunter who is looking for power and deadliness.

CHAPTER XII

HERE is the Winchester definition of trajectory which I quote because it seems as good as any: " The trajectory of a bullet is the path it follows from the time it leaves the muzzle until it strikes the target. This path is a continuous curve. In its flight a bullet loses forward, or horizontal speed, and gains downward or vertical speed."

When a bullet leaves the gun muzzle it begins to drop just the same as though it had been released from the hand. In one second of time during flight the projectile will drop the same distance that it would in the same length of time if allowed to fall from an elevation. Moreover the falling movement is progressive, as pointed out above. It follows then that if the bullet drops a certain distance in say a quarter of a second, it will fall twice that distance in the next quarter, being governed by the laws of gravity exactly as would a falling body without horizontal speed.

Keeping in mind the progressive rate of drop, it will be seen that it would not do to conclude that a rifle with a muzzle velocity of a thousand feet would have a trajectory but twice as high as one with two thousand feet velocity. While the trajectory would of course be governed by the time of the projectile over the course rather than by the initial velocity, yet I can illustrate this point with two well known cartridges.

The .22 long-rifle has a muzzle velocity of 1,103 feet, two hundred yard trajectory, 22 inches. The .30 U. S. A. Krag has a muzzle velocity of 2,000 feet, 200 yard trajectory, 5.41 inches; increase the Krag initial speed to 2,700 and we have a trajectory of 2.85 inches. Hence we can see the importance of gaining every additional hundred feet in muzzle velocity possible if the rifle is to do good work at long, unknown distances.

Trajectory, as measured in inches, is the rise of the bullet above a straight line between the muzzle and center of target, or point of aim, and is usually measured mid-way of the range.

The term "rise of the bullet" is a technical expression, for in reality the bullet never rises above a straight line in extension of the bore of the barrel. The so called rise of the bullet has reference to the " sighting line," the line of vision from the eye across or through the sights and to the target.

Sights are not so set on a rifle as to make the sighting line parallel the bore, but the rear sight is affixed at a higher elevation than the front which causes the path of the bullet's flight to cut the line of sight, or as we say rise above it. If the line of sight really paralleled the line of bore, the bullet would be found to drop lower and lower the longer the range, and never rise above.

As it is, the bullet starts such distance below the line of sight as the front sight is above center of bore; then for some distance the ball travels beneath the line of sight until its path and the " line " converge when it " rises " above. From here on the ball continues to get farther and farther from the line of sight until it reaches a distance about six-tenths of the range, and then the two lines begin closing up until they meet at the center of the target.

The only true point-blank of a rifle is where

the path of the bullet's flight first cuts the line of sight, and this is only a very few yards from the muzzle, depending upon the elevation of the rear sight and the height of front sight above center of bore. The second point-blank, where the bullet again cuts the line of sight, is a variable distance, though we can fix an arbitrary point-blank by saying that a rifle shoots point-blank up to the distance the bullet rises but a slight amount above the line, call it two inches. In practical big game shooting a bullet whose path never leaves the line of sight more than the two inches can be said to be shooting point-blank for the distance.

Trajectory height must not be confused with the drop of the bullet from the straight line in extension of the axis of the bore. For example, a certain rifle with a 2,500 foot muzzle velocity has an eight and a half inch trajectory at three hundred yards, but if we shoot at that three hundred yard target with the rifle sighted for one hundred yards the ball will strike twenty-seven inches below the center. Hence we see the importance of sighting a rifle for the longest distance at which it will not exceed a certain trajectory height, since after we pass the spot at which the sights are aligned the drop of the projectile is very rapid compared with its rise above the sighting line.

The range at which we can fix our arbitrary point-blank, or sight the rifle for hunting, is a matter for the exercise of good judgment. The first thing to be taken into consideration is the initial velocity of the rifle. The .280 Ross and other three thousand foot velocity rifles have trajectories as flat at three hundred yards as the .30-30 has at two hundred; then of course the Ross can be sighted for three hundred yards with no more mid-range error than the .30-30 has at two hundred.

The game at which the weapon is to be used naturally has a bearing on the permissible trajectory height. For deer that are usually shot at distances under two hundred yards, and being small require close holding to reach a vital spot, it would not be wise to tolerate a mid-range error of five inches, the chances being that most of our shots would be taken at just the distance where the bullet was farthest from the line of sight, one hundred to one hundred fifty yards.

However, if the game were of a large variety, like elk, moose, or the larger African antelope, the three thousand foot velocity rifle with a trajectory of five inches at three hundred yards might well be sighted for that distance, and no especial difficulty should be had in holding a trifle low for the mid-ranges. For a deer rifle I should be inclined to place the highest practical trajectory height at four inches. This can be secured from a Ross or 7 mm. Mauser-Spitzer, at 250 yards, from the .30-30 at 165.

With the old-time black powder rifles the size of bull'seye in which the bullet must strike anywhere along its curve of flight was given at eight inches. It might strike the top of the eight-inch bull at one hundred yards and the bottom at two hundred, and the latter distance was supposed to be within the point-blank range of the rifle for big game shooting. However, with modern, high-power arms I should take the size of the bull at six inches, which circle the bullet must not leave up to the maximum distance.

If the rifle is to be sighted for the center of the bull at two hundred yards it is evident that the trajectory must be less than three inches high midway in order to keep within the bull. Such trajectory can be secured from a rifle having a muzzle velocity of 2,600 to 2,700 feet. A rifle with a lower velocity will still keep within the bull by sighting it to strike at six o'clock at two hundred yards in place of in the center.

The difference between the two guns is that the higher velocity will keep within the bull for some distance beyond the stipulated range while the other will not. Thus we can see how flat trajectory very kindly makes amends for bad judgment of distances.

To come down to brass tacks, other things being equal, the trajectory of a big game rifle cannot be too flat. If it has but a one-inch trajectory at two hundred yards that is admirable. Furthermore a six-inch two hundred yard trajectory is the very highest permissible in a high-power rifle for any game. Increasing the muzzle velocity from 2,000 to 3,000 feet lengthens the distance at which the rifle will land in the circle nearly one hundred yards. All this is considered as *other things being equal,* remember.

In black powder days, sacrifices of accuracy, power, and range were made in order to secure flat trajectory. The old principle of sacrificing one essential to secure another still more important might still hold. Let us see. Suppose that in securing our three-inch trajectory at two hundred yards we had to sacrifice accuracy to such an extent that a circle of ten inches would be required to contain a pattern of shots. It is quite evident then that our flat flight would be useless since we could not keep within the given circle in any event. We may, therefore, take it as a simple statement of fact that *trajectory and accuracy must be equal.*

A three-inch trajectory with a ten-inch accuracy pattern is no better than a ten-inch trajectory with a three-inch pattern. But if we can combine a three or four-inch trajectory with a four-inch pattern, we have a great shooting gun—a great shooting gun that might still possibly lack power. I say *might* lack power because a flat trajectory implies power of itself if the bullet is of decent weight and right shape.

It is claimed for the military cartridges, like the '06 Springfield, .280 Ross, 7 mm. Mauser, .25-50 Newton, that they combine in the greatest degree flat trajectory, accuracy, and power. If this is so, and there is not any question at all except as to the power with full mantled Spitzer bullet, they are a wonderful advance in cartridge making.

The power of a cartridge is a multiple of the weight of a bullet and its velocity. Rules for calculating the power of a bullet, given its weight and velocity will not avail much, for the information is generally found in ammunition catalogs, but here is a simple one that may be remembered: Square the given velocity and multiply by the weight of the bullet in one hundred grains and fractions thereof; for example, if the bullet weighs 100 grains multiply by one, if it weighs 250 grains multiply by 2.5. Divide the result by 4,508 and the quotient will be the energy.

Power and energy are almost synonymous terms. Penetration has little to do with the power of a cartridge, but the striking energy is usually taken at a fair measure of the killing qualities, provided the character of the missile is such that it will expend its full force upon the object struck. It follows that the shape and kind of bullet, whether full metal patched, soft-pointed, split-jacketed, or hollow pointed has much to do with the actual execution by a projectile of any given energy.

There is much room for the exercise of good judgment in the choice of a bullet for any particular species of game. First the velocity at which the bullet is to be sent must be taken into consideration. A bullet with a soft point, driven at two thousand feet, might penetrate just right and do good execution; sent at three thousand feet it would possibly expend its force upon the surface and fail to kill, even though its energy were much higher.

At a given velocity a certain kind of bullet may slip though an animal, merely stinging it, while at a higher velocity the ball might have an explosive effect on animal tissue, killing instantly. Diameter of ball is not to be entirely overlooked when considering killing qualities relative to energy. It is generally granted among big game hunters, that given like energy, the missile of largest caliber will have the greatest smashing power.

There is no subject of such perpetual interest to big game hunters as that of the correct shape of bullet to insure its expending its full energy in the right way. The object is, of course, to select a bullet that will penetrate sufficiently and yet expend its entire power on the animal. Naturally if we were shooting deer with a rifle powerful enough for elephants it would not be desirable to have the full energy spent upon the beast unless we wished to make mince meat of it.

Thus we have, in practical results, that the energy of a bullet, governing its killing power, is modified by its shape, character, weight, diameter, velocity, and the animal upon which it is to be used.

ACCURACY AND POWER

ACCURACY AND POWER

Accuracy has been pretty well treated under the head of cartridges and elsewhere but it will do no harm to sum up here. The miniature cartridges should be capable of keeping ten shots in a one-inch circle at fifty yards. In such ammunition velocity and power are not of moment. Small game cartridges should have an accuracy capable of keeping ten shots in a three-inch at one hundred yards, velocity not less than 1,700 feet, and energy of five hundred pounds or better. Deer and antelope ammunition ought to be accurate enough to keep ten shots in a six-inch circle at two hundred yards, with a two hundred trajectory of not greater than six-inches, and striking force of 1,500 foot pounds or more.

Rifles for longer range game work, suitable for moose elk, caribou, mountain sheep, should have an accuracy equal to a six-inch pattern at two hundred yards, or preferably a four trajectory of not greater than a four-inch at two hundred yards, velocity above 2,500 feet, energy from 2,000 to 3,000 foot pounds. Rifles of big bore for long range use should be capable of keeping a string of shots in an eight-inch circle at two hundred yards. Velocity should be from 2,400 to 2,600 feet, with trajectory to correspond. The power would range from three thousand to four thousand foot pounds.

Jungle rifles should be accurate enough to keep ten shots in a ten-inch circle at two hundred yards, velocity from 2,000 to 2,400 feet, energy from four to five thousand pounds. Elephant rifles should keep ten shots in a fifteen-inch, with velocity above two thousand feet, and energy of not less than five thousand foot pounds. In the case of match cartridges it is not worth while to give energy, trajectory, or velocity and they will be omitted from the table.

Most of the figures in the ballistic table which follows are taken from the catalogs of the Winchester and U. M. C. companies and may be accepted as correct. The ballistics of English cartridges are taken from the catalogs of Jeffery, Greener, and Westley-Richards. Usually their statements are rather indefinite, being about so and so—they fail to supply figures for free recoil, and that had to be calculated. Some of the figures for foreign cartridges I have secured from the American agents and I cannot vouch for their correctness. Probably they are approximately true.

It is human nature for a manufacturer to make the best possible showing for his arms and ammunition. For example, one agent who had a rifle giving a muzzle velocity of 2,900 feet gave the trajectory as considerably flatter than that of another rifle with similar weight and shape of bullet, having a speed of 3,100 feet; some builders with rifles having ballistics similar to the '06 gave the free recoil as about half the '06—in that case I had to do some guessing myself. Free recoil of automatic arms cannot be obtained in any instance.

BALLISTIC TABLE.

Cartridge.	Weight, bullet, grains.	Muzzle velocity, ft. sec.	Muzzle eg, ft. lbs.	100 yard trajectory in.	Accuracy 200 yards circle.	Free recoil, ft. lbs.	
6 mm. Navy	112	2,562	1,632	3.49	6 in.	7.10	
.22 Newton	70	2,750	1,158	3.	6 "	4.	
.25-20 S. S.	86	1,411	380	13.52	6 "	.51	
.25-20 H. P.	86	1,712	560	9.37	8 "	1.36	
.25-30 Win.	117	2,030	1,070	6.	6 "	3.39	
.25 Newton	117	3,500	3,179	1.50	6 "	10.	
.280 Ross	145	3,100	3.090	2.	4 "	16.	est.
7 mm. Mauser. (Spitzer)	139	2,920	2,628	2.25	6 "	15.	est.
7 mm. Mauser. (Spitzer)	154	2,871	2,815	2.50	6 "	19.	est.
Springfield ('06)	150	2,700	2,425	2.85	4 "	14.	
.30-40 Krag	220	2,005	1,972	5.41	6 "	11.59	
.30-30 Marlin	170	2,008	1,522	5.79	6 "	7.20	
.32 Special	170	2,112	1,684	5.60	6 "	7.66	
.33 Win.	200	2,056	1,877	5.78	6 "	11.35	
.275-203 (Axite)	215	2,500	3,000	3.50	6 "	20.	est.
.318 W. R. (Axite)	250	2,400	3,194	4.	6 "	24.	est.
.351 Win. (Self-loader)	180	1,861	1,523	7.60	8 "		
.333 Jeffery	250	2,600	4,000	3.	6 "	35.	est.
.35 Win.	250	2,200	2,687	4.73	6 "	19.81	
.35 Rem. S. L.	200	2,000	1,776	5.40	6 "		
.401 Win. (S. L.)	200	2,141	2,033	6.47	8 "		
.401 Win. (S. L.)	250	1,875	1,952	7.34	8 "		
.405 Win.	300	2,204	3,236	4.85	6 "	28.24	
.404 Jeffery	400	2,200	4,000	4.75	8 "	44.	
.450 Jeffery	480	2,200	5,000	4.75	10 "	50.	est.
.475 Jeffery	500	2,150	5,000	5.	12 "	55.	est.
.577 Greener	750	2,050	5.680	5.6	12 "	55.	est.
.600 Jeffery	900	2,050	8,700	5.4	15 "	100.	est.

CHAPTER XIII

ONE of our rifle building companies states in their catalog that as a rule a rifle will shoot three inches higher at one hundred yards when shot with a muzzle rest than it will when fired off-hand. This simple statement is worth considering and analyzing in these days of light weight, heavily charged arms.

The average novice naturally concludes that when his piece is properly sighted for the distance, with no wind to affect the flight of the bullet, and he holds dead on and pulls trigger without a wobble, something is due to happen to the target. But if the deer runs away with his flag up, or the bull'seye shows no bullet hole, he humbly accepts the blame with the hope of making amends next time. However, one of the first things he needs to learn is that the rifle may be as accurate as any ever built, the sighting, holding, and pulling perfect, and yet the ball may obstinately refuse to go to the desired spot.

There are reasons for this which we cannot

119

treat at length in this chapter, but one is light. For example a hold at 6 o'clock may be placing the bullets in the center with one light, but a change in light will possibly throw the projectile above the bull or beneath it. Again a change in temperature has its influence, and, moreover, the rifle that has been sighted near sea level will not shoot on the same elevation when in the mountains several thousand feet higher. What we wish to emphasize here, though, is that the manner of holding the weapon, and the position of the marksman in shooting may cause a wide variation of the bullet on the target—due entirely to recoil.

This is not a scientific disquisition on rifle shooting, nevertheless the bearing of recoil upon accurate rifle work is so pronounced and so unavoidable that every man who uses a rifle at all should understand it and guard against it as far as he may. In the first place, under the influence of powder gas, a rifle barrel expands; in the next place it may bend, technically called " flip; " third, it may " jump " or rise, and lastly it may move to one side or the other—all this after the marksman has completed his work of sighting, holding, and pulling trigger, and while the bullet is moving from breech to muzzle.

WEIGHT AND RECOIL

The principles that govern are: The lighter the rifle and the heavier the charge, the worse will it jump or flip. Long, slender barrels flip, while short barrels jump. Long, military fore-stocks running to nearly the end of the barrel lessen flip, but may injure the accuracy through binding the tube and preventing expansion. Rifles that are shot with like charges, from like positions, held with like force or grip, jump or flip uniformly, in which case the movement might be ignored.

Our military authorities once experimented to see how heavy a Springfield .45-70-500 barrel would have to be in order to reach a maximum of accuracy. They were trying to reach a weight of barrel so heavy that it would not move while the bullet was passing from breech to muzzle. They learned that the most accurate work could be accomplished only with a barrel weighing about thirty pounds. Even that weight could not be held rigidly without deflecting the ball, but must be allowed to move backward with the recoil, backed up by the shoulder or a spring. When the barrel was confined, as in a vise, a weight of one hundred pounds was demanded if accuracy was considered. A further surprising discovery was that the thirty-pound barrel gave a considerably higher velocity than one of normal weight.

Further experiments with the .45 and a certain weight of barrel showed that loading the cartridge with a five hundred grain bullet for one shot and a three hundred and fifty grain for the next, the heavy ball, which should in reason have gone the lowest, landed four inches higher than the other at fifty yards. Our combination rifles, those handling black powder and lead bullets, also smokeless powder and mantled bullets with a higher velocity, cannot be shot with the same alignment of sights—the high-pressure charge will "kick" its bullet away above the other. I have found that the lightly loaded .32-40-165 would shoot six inches higher at two hundred yards when shot with a muzzle rest than when held off-hand, this with an arm weighing over ten pounds. The same rifle would show a variation of three or four inches when shot off-hand, depending on whether it was held tightly or simply allowed to hang in the hands.

A .30-40 weight 7½ pounds threw its bullets ten inches higher with a muzzle rest than it did off-hand. The .32-40, it should be kept in mind, is a weapon of very light recoil, 3.08 foot pounds. What a rifle with thirty pounds of recoil would do under a like test, the Lord knows, at least I do not.

Not only is there a variation in the landing point of the bullet when shot with a rest and off-hand, but there will be a change, either vertical or horizontal, every time the rifleman adopts a new position or a different style of holding. The rifle shot from the knee rest, for instance, may shoot high or it may place its bullets to one side or the other. The sitting position will probably again necessitate a change in the sighting. Even shooting the weapon with extended arm, or with body rest and guard in the palm will make a difference in elevation.

Probably the two positions that shoot the nearest to one elevation are the off-hand and the prone. It is not likely with either of these that there would be enough variation to cause missing of game though for fine target work the sights would have to be changed.

The gist of all this is that if the hunter has a rifle of high power and heavy recoil he should devote a great deal of study to its idiosyncracies. A rifle of recoil above twenty-five pounds can never be shot with accuracy from any description of rest that might be resorted to in the game field, and as a consequence the sportsman must

never be tempted to rest his piece for the sake
of a more secure aim, if he does the result will
be a certain and outrageous miss regardless of
how well he may have held. Unless the owner
has tested his piece thoroughly in the three common positions used in game shooting, off-hand,
knee-rest, and prone, and knows just how much
the sighting should be varied, he had better confine himself to the off-hand, no matter if he cannot hold so steadily. The bullet will at least
land where he pulls it and that is something it
may not do with any other style of holding.

Where time and opportunity serve, however,
the hunter should practice with his weapon until
he knows it by heart. He can then, without
change of sight, vary his holding enough to make
allowance for the effect of recoil in the position
he finds most opportune.

If the rifle shoots to the right from the knee
rest, something it is quite likely to do, why hold
a trifle to the left every time you kneel to shoot.
If it shoots low in the prone or high, be sure to
find it out and exactly how much. In passing,
it might be well to state here that the man who
can keep ten shots in the eight-inch circle at two
hundred yards, shooting one shot from the prone,
one from the knee, and one standing, following

it up in regular rotation, possesses a higher order of rifle skill than he who could keep his ten straight in the bull off-hand.

It is a common thing to discover that a rifle will not shoot the same for two different people without change of sights. This is usually ascribed to difference in vision, which of course might be true, but often it is a mere matter of whether or not the weapon is pressed firmly to the shoulder and how it is gripped. One of the hardest lessons to learn in rifle shooting is that of grasping and backing up the piece uniformly. If under excitement and nervous strain the marksman tightens his grip upon the arm to an unusual extent, the result will surely be noted on the target.

Everything here said applies emphatically to heavily charged rifles of light weight. It requires a high order of skill indeed to shoot a .450 high-power rifle, and few are the men who can make a good pattern with it whatever the position from which it is shot. More than one sharpshooter can keep his ten shots in the six-inch at two hundred yards with the Scheutzen .28 who could not stay in the three-foot circle with the Jeffery .333. Hence we have the axiomatic advice, be sure in the first place that you are buying a rifle that you can *hit* something with, and afterwards consider other qualities.

The gallery rifles, .22 short and .22 long-rifle, have respectively about a tenth of a pound and a quarter of a pound of free recoil, this with an average weight of rifle of ten pounds. A gun of this kind should shoot nearly to the same center, however it might be held. The Schuetzen .28-30-120 has, I should estimate, a recoil of two pounds and the .32-40 three pounds. The marksman would have to be very sensitive who would object to this, and yet the arms have to be grasped very uniformly, with the hands in like position every time in order to maintain an even elevation. The guns from which these cartridges are shot usually weigh from twelve to fifteen pounds. The principal utility of the heavy tube is a negative recoil, to prevent the barrel from being moved by the pressure of the charge while the bullet is passing to the muzzle.

While the finest rest shooting has been accomplished with a heavy rifle having a recoil of six foot pounds, yet such a piece has been considered as having too great a kick for the best work off-hand. We thus see that the finest results in off-hand shooting demand a rifle with not over a quarter of a pound of recoil to the pound weight of the rifle; even a half pound to the pound weight of the gun would be objectionable.

In game rifles, though, some sacrifice of hair-splitting accuracy must be made. Few men would be willing to carry a hunting arm weighing above ten pounds and many go to the other extreme, asking for a six-pound weapon or lighter. A recoil of a foot pound to the pound weight of the arm should scarcely be felt in actual game shooting, though it might strike people as unpleasantly assertive in a match rifle or one from which a large number of shots were to be fired.

This proportion of pound for pound would give very high pattern values with reference to the holding. This weight of recoil relative to arm can be had practically in the various cartridges from .30-30 to .33 Winchester and .35 Remington. Anyone who can shoot a game rifle at all should be able to fire these cartridges without flinching, or scattering his bullets through inability to hold a kicking rifle steadily.

In the next class of weapons, like those of the .30-40 Springfield '06, .280 Ross, 8 mm. Mauser, .35 Winchester, we have from two to three pounds of recoil to the pound weight of the rifle. Not one man in fifty can shoot such arms well without special training in their use. With these weapons the slingstrap will be found of considerable assistance in controlling the piece *while the bullet is passing out of the barrel.* Once a marksman has become inured to the recoil and has learned how to control it and make allowance for its effects, these are among our finest and most accurate game cartridges. Nevertheless, it is not to be disputed that many men will never learn to handle these guns and cartridges so effectively as they would those of less power.

Guns of four to five pounds of recoil to the pound weight of the arm, including the .405 Winchester, .333 Jeffery, .318 Westley-Richards, 9 mm, Mannlicher, .375 cordite, are weapons which require considerable skill to shoot well with in more than one position. For the ordinary marksman it will be found wise to attempt to shoot these rifles only in the off-hand and the knee-rest. Even then he should not expect to accomplish what a rifleman would consider really fine work, though his game hits will make up in power what they lack in accuracy. These are specialized game cartridges, neither adapted to the average man nor to general service. He who could make a good diagram with them at two hundred yards would have reason to congratulate himself on a performance that is quite beyond the capabilities of most men.

The .400, .404, .450, .475, and .500 cordite are *big* game rifles to be used on animals of the largest size, or in stopping dangerous beasts at short ranges. It is not expected that the hunter will be able to shoot accurately at long range with these arms. Except the weapons are made very heavy, they have a free recoil of from five to seven pounds to the pound weight of the rifle, and along with it a severe concussion. A Sir Samuel Baker or a Roosevelt could handle them and a few other men who are as kindly endowed by nature.

Two classes of sportsmen might consider the purchase of these arms, one those who are liable to be placed in the path of a charging lion, and the other the men who can take a heavily loaded ten bore shotgun, weighing eight pounds, and shoot off both barrels at once with a deliberate aim, time after time, without betraying any tendency to flinch. Having undergone this test, try the rifle at a mark and if the two hundred yard diagram of ten shots is satisfactory, buy it. If I had to shoot the elephant rifle with its charge of one hundred grains of powder and nine hundred grain bullet it would only be in case of life or death anyhow, at one end or the other.

Table giving minimum weight of rifles for proper proportion of charge and recoil.

.30-30 Winchester should weigh	. . . .	7	pounds
.303 Savage " "	. . . .	7	"
.30 Automatic " "	. . . .	7	"
.32 Special	. . . .	7	
.33 Winchester	. . . .	7½	
.35 Remington	. . . .	7½	
.30-40 Krag	. . . .	8	
.401 Winchester " "	. . . .	8	
.30-40 Army '06 " "	. . . .	8½	
.280 Ross	. . . .	8½	
7 mm. Mauser	. . . .	8½	
8 mm. Mauser	. . . .	8½	
.35 Winchester	. . . .	8½	
.405 Winchester " "	. . . .	9	
.218 Axite	. . . .	9	
.333 Jeffery	. . . .	9	
.11 mm. Mauser " "	. . . .	10	
.50-110 Winchester " "	. . . .	10	
.400 Jeffery "	. . . .	11	
.404 Jeffery "	. . . .	11	
.475 Cordite	. . . .	12	
.500 Holland	. . . .	12	
.500 Greener	. . . .	13	
.577 Magnum	. . . .	15	
.600 Jeffery	. . . .	20	
4 bore	. . . .	20	

Note that for the English cartridges double rifles are frequently built of about the weights given here; single barrel and bolt-action rifles are generally lighter, being frequently too light for comfort and accuracy. Foreign bolt rifles are as a rule light of weight relative to charge. Our own arms are constructed near the weights given, often a trifle heavier, though we have some featherweights.

TESTING ACCURACY AND ALIGNMENT OF SIGHT

The make up of a cartridge and the reputation of the builders of a rifle are a pretty good general guarantee of its accuracy. From some cartridges greater accuracy is to be expected than from others, and some manufacturers have a worldwide reputation for the close shooting of their rifles. Nevertheless, not all arms of a certain caliber and make will show equally fine diagrams. Nearly every weapon will probably do good average work, but occasionally one will be found capable of shooting wonderful patterns, and just as surely there will be an odd gun now and then that is a bad performer. Tests at the factory cannot always be depended upon to detect the poor barrel, hence it is well to be able to test the shooting of a gun ourselves.

The best way to target a rifle that the writer has discovered is to make a neat fitting box to sit in, having a firm rest for the back and side pieces for the arms to rest upon. Have the box strongly made and immovable. Place a bag of sand across the front of the box and dent a place into this where the barrel is to be placed—sand bag to be at such a distance as to rest the barrel about six inches from the muzzle. Hold down firmly with the left hand when you fire and do not vary the grip from shot to shot.

Place the bull'seye at the distance you wish the rifle sighted for and hold just under the black, where the bullets should land in the center. Do not expect to secure the finest work the barrel is capable of even with this rest; perfection in rest shooting requires training and a lot of it. Endeavor to call every shot and make due allowance for bad holding, the effect of wind, etc.

Remember that the character of the sights will make quite a difference in the resulting diagrams. With the ordinary open hunting sights ten shots in about a ten-inch circle would be as good as an inexperienced man could expect to do. Globe and peep sights might narrow the circle to eight inches, and with telescope, after enough practice, to six. Finer work than this would necessitate much training on the part of the marksman or a machine rest.

If the weapon maintains an even elevation but the shots spread laterally, I would be inclined to consider it the marksman's own fault or that of the wind. If the bullets simply scatter about over the target, as a general thing the fault lies with the shooter. Where the elevation is irregular the trouble might be in the way the marksman is gripping his gun, or the barrel may be wrong. When the piece plays a number of bullets in one group and then changes to a spot some inches away and begins grouping again, condemn the barrel; there is little you can do for it. If the barrel shoots well, except that it throws an occasional wild shot, it is more than likely that the ammunition is to blame.

Never rest the rifle against anything solid or attempt to confine it rigidly in any way when testing for accuracy. An eight-inch bull at two hundred yards will be found about the right thing for open or peep sights, a telescope might be aligned on something much smaller. Naturally the distance at which you test the piece would be governed by its caliber and the purpose for which you intend to use the gun. Generally big game rifles are targeted at two hundred yards, small game at one hundred, and miniature at fifty yards or for gallery use at seventy-five feet.

ALIGNMENT OF SIGHTS

If the arm shoots high or low, it is a simple matter to correct that with the usual adjustable sights. Bear in mind, however, that the rifle should shoot higher with the rest than it would when the barrel touched nothing. After the sights are properly aligned with a rest, a few shots in the off-hand will give the correct elevation for that style of shooting.

Should the rifle shoot to one side or the other, first see that the front sight is exactly over the center of bore, after which do not touch it again but turn your attention to the rear sight for the correction of further errors. If the rifle is shooting to the left move the rear sight to the right, and vice versa. Usually such sight can be moved in its slot, the slightest movement probably being sufficient. When you get it right be sure the sight is tight enough not to be moved by any accidental jar.

If the Lyman or other tang sight doesn't shoot to center place a piece of paper under one side and cant the sight over in the direction you wish the bullets to go. Of course if the sight has a wind gauge, that can be moved the most readily, but as a rule adjust correctly in the first place without the use of the gauge, and then it will be easier to read windage from zero afterwards.

CHAPTER XIV

STOCKS AND TRIGGERS

FACTORY built rifles of standard dimensions, especially all the old models, are too short in the stock. There is no good reason why a man should use a fourteen-inch stock on his shotgun and but thirteen for the rifle. The rifle, being shot more deliberately as a rule, would, if anything, permit the longer stock. With a long stock the recoil is apparently less severe than with a short one, probably because the kick is caught by the shoulder rather than the face. Certain positions in rifle firing, as the hip and body rest, favor short stocks, but with arm extended, as a hunter should shoot, stocks should be of like length with those used on the shotgun.

In its drop the rifle stock would be dependent a good deal on the sights used; a telescope mounted high above the barrel necessitates a raised comb. Ordinarily the comb of a rifle will be higher in proportion to heel drop than we find on a shotgun.

A man doesn't assume the same attitude in shooting the rifle as with the shotgun, standing erect in place of leaning over his gun. For this reason the rifleman requires a greater drop at heel in proportion to comb. The average marksman would be suited with a rifle having a stock fourteen inches long, comb one and one-half inches for open sights, one inch for telescope; heel three inches. More drop might be demanded in some instances; ease and grace of posture should always be studied, without any contortion of shoulder, neck, or face to make the stock fit. I believe the worst fault in the general run of stocks is a low and sharp comb. Then when the rear sight is elevated the face is carried quite away from the wood and when the rifle jumps with the shot the comb gets in an uppercut on the chin.

CHEEK-PIECE

A cheekpiece is something that I particularly like in a rifle, and I think that every one of good grade or made to order should have it. It gives a firmer hold of the weapon, tends to confidence, and prevents flinching, and, moreover, resting the head takes a strain off the neck, which strain in turn affects the muscles of the eyes.

I must emphasize this eye-strain that comes

from cramping the muscles of the neck and trying to hold the head still at the same time. Few men can throw the face forward and hold it there for any length of time, unsupported, without feeling a strain on the back of the neck which seems to have a pulling effect on the sighting eye. Keep this strain up long enough and the muscles of the eye begin to quiver. I have known instances in deliberate Schuetzen work where rolling sparkles of light seemed to pass before the eye. This strain on unsupported muscles is the main reason a telescope mounted on the side of a barrel is worse than none.

From the foregoing it may be inferred that a cheekpiece is absolutely essential to deliberate and accurate rifle firing in the off-hand position. With the face resting firmly on a cheekpiece of the right height and shape, all strain is taken from the neck and eye and the cheek is lifted by the recoil in place of being struck a blow. Very few people contract the fatal habit of flinching from shoulder punishment, but a blow in the face will cause any but a pugilist to bat his eye.

HIGH GRADE OF WOOD AND ITS ORNAMENTATION

Beauty of wood is no less desirable in a rifle than in a shotgun. Of the two weapons the rifle will generally receive the less hard usage, and it is eminently fit that it should be an arm of both beauty and utility. A handsomely checkered and carved walnut stock of selected grain and fine finish is a fit source of pride for any sportsman. Further, in the carving and finish of their gun-stocks, our great rifle building firms turn out an arm fully equal to the best hand-made shotguns of Continental Europe and superior to any built in England.

The prices, too, being moderate, there is no good reason, so far as the writer can perceive, why a rifleman should not give full rein to his esthetic tastes when purchasing his grooved arm. It is true that beauty of wood adds nothing to the actual utility of the arm, just as a darkey wench can bake as good pancakes as anybody if that were all you asked for in a wife.

ENGRAVING

What has been said of ornamenting stocks is emphatically true of the engraving to be had on our high grade factory rifles. The style of engraving which can be placed upon a rifle by our big factories is superior to the best found on American shotguns, and not excelled, if equaled, anywhere in the world. It is cleverly designed, beautifully executed, highly artistic—something in which every American citizen can take a patriotic pride. The fact that the standard rifle will shoot as well as any has little bearing, for so will a $25 shotgun perform fully up to one costing $500, yet few of us select the cheap gun if we can afford a better in finish.

FRAMES AND FITTING

In repeating rifles no such hairlike fitting of steel to steel, characteristic of high grade shotguns, is possible. However, bolts and locking lugs, sears, springs, and other parts should be of the best material, highly polished and smoothly adjusted, while the frames should be skilfully and thoroughly casehardened. In the standard guns which sell from fifteen to twenty dollars we cannot expect much hand adjustment, but in the better grades we are entitled to this. Frequently a competent gunsmith can add to the smooth working of bolts and levers, and his services in touching up trigger-pulls, reducing springs that may be too stiff, etc., may render a new rifle much more satisfactory.

BUTT-PLATES

The thirteen-inch rifle stock and the crescent

shaped butt-plate seem to be a survival from flint lock days. More and more a preference is being shown for shotgun butts. Undoubtedly in high-power or big bore rifles, where the recoil exceeds fifteen pounds, a shotgun butt is by all means to be preferred. It should be preferably broader and deeper than that of a shotgun so as to distribute the force over the shoulder, and where the recoil is above thirty pounds it would be well to fit a recoil pad. With a rifle shot deliberately, as at the target, recoil is always felt to twice the extent that it is in snap shooting, and few find it pleasant to have a sharp, narrow butt driven into the shoulder.

Nevertheless, with a repeating rifle of the lever-action type, which the marksman expects to function rapidly while the butt is at the shoulder, the crescent butt is the proper thing. It clings to the shoulder without the tendency to slip down that a straight plate would have, and the hunter can continue to fire rapidly without the necessity of readjusting the rifle to his shoulder for every shot. I think, too, that where snap-shots are to be taken with a rifle the eye is more likely to take the sights instantly with the crescent butt, the stock coming more uniformly to shoulder and cheek. However, this is not important enough to warrant much consideration where the recoil of the arm is severe.

Schuetzen and Swiss buttplates are quite out of place on a hunting rifle, or any other rifle that is to be shot with the left arm extended—they have their uses, but not on a game rifle. I do not like hard rubber buttplates on a rifle; they wear too smooth and slip. Have the plate of steel, checkered rough. It is a simple job for the rifleman to do the checkering himself if he likes.

PISTOL OR STRAIGHT GRIP

Many prefer a pistol grip for the reason that they are accustomed to it—it is more homelike. However, when the weapon has a loop-lever or a finger lever, either of which is better than any pistol grip, I see no utility in the curved " hand." The loop-lever is a splendid aid in pulling a heavy trigger, it being possible to give a backward pressure to the hand which can be transferred to the pulling finger without contracting it greatly. The finger lever is just about as good in this respect as the loop. Where the fingers are tightly clasping the grip, an effort to press the trigger may merely tighten the other fingers, thus affecting the holding, and at the same time delaying the let-off past the exact instant when the trigger should yield.

In double rifles and bolt-action guns the pistol grip might be of some advantage. But it should be of a decided sort, well curved in toward the guard, and not a mere ugly lump somewhere back of the actual grip, the kind we often see on lever-action rifles.

SLINGSTRAPS

The slingstrap is not only the right thing for carrying a rifle on long tramps, but as a support for the forward arm it is nearly as good as the German "hand-hold." It can be used in other positions as well as in the off-hand, and in any of them it assists in the steady holding of the piece while taking up considerable recoil. It might be in the way sometimes when traveling through brush or for quick shots, but its benefits quite outweigh its drawbacks. With any heavily charged rifle I should strongly advise a sling-strap.

TRIGGERS AND TRIGGER PULL

Rifle triggers may be plain of pull, as in a shotgun, single set trigger or double set. The single set trigger I have never liked on any rifle for any purpose. In its mechanism this trigger pushes well forward to set, and then, as it yields to pressure and releases the sear, returns to its original position, the trigger and finger movement being so great as to disturb the aim, I have never yet seen a single set trigger that did not have a variable pull, at one time yielding with half the pressure that it might on a second attempt. The result need not be dwelt upon; the marksman becomes afraid to touch his trigger, not being able to gauge the weight at which it will yield, and the consequence is a slower let-off than with a hard, plain trigger, as well as many premature pulls.

The double set trigger is admirably adapted to certain purposes, but should never be used on a heavily charged big game rifle; any arm with a pronounced recoil needs to be held, not tight but firmly, and it is a difficult task to put on a grip with the entire hand except the forefinger which is to barely touch a hair trigger. When the gun is swung rapidly for a snap-shot, or under excitement, the result is nearly certain to be disastrous. Nothing so rattles a hunter in moments of stress or danger as a premature discharge of his weapon; for dangerous game anything in the shape of a set trigger is not to be considered.

For small game rifles, single-shots, and those used exclusively at the target, by all means a double set trigger, but stop at that and never place it on your big game hunting rifle.

The trigger of a game rifle should be smooth, without drag, or any more " give " than is necessary to release the sear. The trigger pull should be from three to five pounds, depending upon the weight, caliber, and recoil of the arm. I have never seen the need of a trigger pull heavier than five pounds, even on a military rifle, and four pounds is enough. The trigger should yield to the ounce, though, time after time. Giving with a three pound pressure for one shot and five the next is a fatal defect.

No matter what quality a rifle may have, if the trigger pull is bad the arm is not fit to place faith in. I have noticed that plain triggers with a very light pull, say two and a half pounds and under, are more likely to be variable than those that are harder. A regular seven pound pull is odds better than one that lets go from two pounds up.

The marksman of a mechanical turn can generally improve his trigger pull by careful work with an oil stone, testing the let-off frequently while at work by attaching a weight to the trigger. Should he find either the sear or hammer soft, after adjusting the pull to his taste, take the pieces to a gunsmith and have them hardened. It not infrequently happens with cheap rifles that the parts will be found too soft to retain a perfect release, especially if it is light.

CHAPTER XV

RIFLE SIGHTS

THE sights have been called the eye of the rifle. Certainly the most powerful big game weapon would be but a blind giant without them. Proper sights for the work in hand contribute to the success of any rifleman, though the man with youthful and normal eyesight finds other problems, like holding, judging distance, and trigger pulling, much more difficult than actually sighting his piece.

The old pioneer long-rifleman had the simplest sights, consisting of a silver or copper bead and a straight bar, notched rear, often without any means of elevating, yet their work within the range of those rifles was hardly inferior to what we see to-day. It is a pretty well established tradition that in an early day a market shooter of Illinois killed one hundred and twenty deer in the month of October, firing but one hundred and fifty shots. His rifle shot bullets of forty to the pound and the longest kill was made at four hundred yards.

About the best deer shot that I ever happened to run across was a swamp-colored Arkansawyer carrying a Winchester .44 upon which he had fixed home-made sights, a front bead made from a bear's tooth, the rear a straight iron bar, wedge shaped, tapered to an edge at the top, notched, and blackened. There was no provision made for elevation and neither need there be for use in the woods. The veteran assured me that at one hundred and fifty yards he would kill his buck with a single bullet oftener than he'd miss it, and this range he seemed to consider about the maximum distance for shooting in heavy timber.

A skilled rifleman can shoot well with any sort of sights; line up two pins on top of the barrel and he will get along nicely. Nevertheless there are special sights adapted to special purposes and the province of this chapter is to point them out and tell what they are good for and why.

Rifle sights might be classed roughly as open-sights, peep, globe, military, and telescope. We can dismiss the military sights now with the statement that if the reader is a military man he must use such sights as the Government stipulates whether he likes them or not. Military sights are well adapted to the purpose for which they were invented, and they will do very well for game shooting—fully as well as, but no better than, the ordinary open sight.

OPEN FRONT SIGHTS

Front beads and other foresights are manufactured in great variety. We have the plain Rocky Mountain knife-blade front, and then ivory beads of various shapes and sizes, gold beads, platinum, and different combinations. Marble's front sight in one model has a reversible bead, one end showing ivory and the other gold. King's front sight rolls over, turning one bead down and another up,—it is called triple bead because of its three beads of various styles. Beach and Lyman also make foresights that are a combination of ivory bead and a pinhead with hood; these last do best service on a rifle that is mostly used for shooting at a mark.

Sights are much a matter of individual liking and habitual use. If I express a personal preference it need not be considered an edict of the Medes and Persians. I believe that a rifle intended for big game shooting will as a rule be subjected to considerable rough usage. It may be carried miles on horseback or in the bottom of a boat or in a wagon. Sights then should be of the strongest and plainest, without any combinations, windgauges, reversibles— nothing but the plain bead in its steel setting, no frills or hollow rims, holes beneath or hoods above. Leave all such things to the theorist, the man who does his rifle shooting on the club-house veranda.

The ivory bead can be obtained either square or round and of sizes from the big " jack-sight " to the smallest beads that should be used by a hunter. Many have a preference for the square bead, but its sharp corners sparkle in the sun and not as fine work can be accomplished with it under all conditions. The Sheard gold bead has many admirers and much merit.

I believe that the generality of sportsmen will agree with me that one or the other of these two front sights, ivory or gold, should be found on a hunting rifle, and taboo combinations, also windgauges for such weapons.

OPEN REAR SIGHTS

Open rear sights are generally preferred for

running shots, snap-shots, and all work where it is imperative that a quick and clear view of the game be, not obtained, but retained. Where a bounding deer tops the brush but a time or two and is gone, any description of peep sight is useless, and where dangerous game is liable to charge they would be foolish. Hence while the finest match work cannot be secured with open sights, yet they are generally chosen as the most practical for game shooting, especially big game.

No less an authority than Theodore Van Dyke preferred a straight narrow bar without a notch for a rear sight. My own experience is that this will do very well for snap work but is not accurate enough for deliberate shooting. The ordinary Winchester sporting rear is about as good as any of those with all kinds of patents attached. I like the model known as the " flat top," the top but slightly crescent shaped. A deep crescent, like the deep notch, will reflect the light from one side or the other, and is difficult to get down into where the eye has no time to hunt for the rear sight notch.

If the bar is quite straight the shooter may not get the center in rapid aiming; his doing so would depend upon the fit of his rifle stock. The sporting rear sight has a ready means of elevation and alignment for different distances. Its one serious defect is that it cannot be used to advantage where the rifle carries a peep sight on tang or receiver, but should then be replaced by the folding leaf rear sight.

Beware of the rear sight with a platinum line marking the center. This bright line looks good in theory but in practice, in some lights, it will blend with the ivory of the front bead so that you cannot readily tell how much of the bead is being taken—in a hurried shot the bead might not be seen at all, the eye being deceived by the platinum line. Let the rear bar be plain, solid, and as black as you can get it. Any diamond shaped or circular hole through the bar beneath the notch merely adds to the blur and lets in light where it can do no good. A hood over the rear sight is detrimental to quick work, takes the sight out of its class, and makes a makeshift target sight of it.

THE FOLDING LEAF REAR SIGHT

The folding leaf sight is that in common use on English express rifles, one leaf turning down and another up for different ranges. The folding leaf will accomplish everything that can be done with the sporting rear and has the further advantage of folding flat down on the barrel when not needed.

The English manner of using the folding leaf is that commonly followed in the muzzleloading days of fixed sights, taking more or less of the front bead according to the range. With this system a fine sight would be taken for short distances, a coarser bead at medium, and the full bead further out; at longer ranges even the stem of the front sight might be used to secure the elevation.

This system of aiming has its advantages and disadvantages. The trajectory of the bullet can be gauged very readily and learned thoroughly. However, it really implies holding over for the longer ranges, and if the bead is a large one it may entirely cover the game or hide the spot to be struck. Most marksmen would rather sight the piece to shoot center at its longest flat trajectory range, and then hold a trifle under for mid distances. Either system is better than trying to set the sight for every little variation in range. Open rear sights are hardly to be relied upon beyond the second point blank of the rifle. If the rifle is intended for very long ranges have a rear peep and fold the leaf down out of the way.

RIFLE SIGHTS

A peep sight is simply a hole in a bar of iron through which to aim. The larger the hole the quicker and clearer the sight; the smaller the orifice the greater the accuracy. The size of the peep hole might be regulated by individual eyes, also by the uses to be made of the sight. Hunters prefer a large peep and target shots a small one. Generally speaking, large apertures go with coarse beads and the reverse.

While the sighting principle is the same, rear peep sights are of different shapes and models, affixed in various positions. Peep sights have been tried upon the barrel in the position of the ordinary rear or middle sight, but they are then too far from the eye; even with large aperture the field is too small. The Marble, Lyman, and Vernier tang sights are screwed to the tang, and the upright arm is hinged so that it may be folded down out of the way. I have no space to describe these sights fully, but any catalog will do that.

The Vernier is the most accurate because of its disc-cup which cuts off the side light, but it cuts off all the field except that seen through the aperture and is not fit for a hunting rifle. The

153

Lyman and the Marble Combination peep sights are compact and have been especially designed for hunting rifles. Both the Marble and the Lyman have two apertures, the plate of the smaller fitting inside the larger. Ordinarily the smaller aperture would be used for deliberate work and the other for quick, that is in theory. As a matter of fact the shooter in actual hunting must make up his mind to use one aperture or the other, rarely having time to make a change in the presence of game.

From my own personal experience I do not like the two aperture combination; the narrow one is too small for running shots and the larger too coarse for accuracy—one medium sized aperture would be better than the two. The claim is made by the manufacturers of these sights that the eye always instinctively takes the center of an aperture, but I have not found this true. On the other hand, the man who has been accustomed to open sights will from habit get down into the bottom of the aperture just as he has been accustomed to with the notch of the bar sight. The result is invariably a lower line of elevation for the large peep. Only where the aperture is small will the eye take the center uniformly and then there is no instinct about it.

for the only clear light comes through the middle.

Many profess to be able to do better snap work with a large aperture than with any description of bar sight, but I have always found a peep slow because the first thing to be done is to fit the eye to the aperture, and meantime perhaps the game disappears. Of course tin cans might be sighted upon in the air, also rabbits or deer running in the open, but not game that must be taken instantaneously. If anyone believes that I am wrong, let him try an aperture on his shotgun for quail shooting. It might be well to note that no professional snap and trick shot uses peep sights.

The sportsman whose eyes are becoming "long-sighted" will probably learn that he can no longer do his holding skill justice with a bar sight, but must use a peep. In that case the bar should be removed, or folded down if a leaf, and the small aperture plate knocked out—narrow peeps are trying to old eyes.

Tang peep sights find their greatest utility upon lightly charged rifles, without the intermediate bar. To bring the bar into service the peep has to be folded down; there it spoils the grip to such an extent that I would rather have the gun without it. Moreover, the sight is too close to the eye and always liable to injure it where the piece has a heavy recoil. For use on a high-power arm the " receiver " sight should replace the tang peep. As its name implies this sight is fastened to the receiver of the rifle where it is quite out of the way of the hand, and, since it is in no way inferior to the other, should be given the preference for a hunting rifle.

The best all round combination of sights that I know of for game shooting is an ivory or gold front bead, a middle folding leaf bar with a U shaped notch, and a receiver peep. The receiver sight should be so fitted that when run down to the lowest point it will be under the line of vision across the bar. Have the bar aligned for short range and the peep for two hundred yards. Keep the leaf folded flat except when a snap-shot is probable and then turn the peep out of the way.

Where the rear peep is to be used in match shooting, other appliances furthering fine aiming are demanded; as, globe front with pinhead or aperture, windgauge, spirit level, micrometer elevating screw, and eye-cup with adjustable apertures for difference in light. However, peep sights have about seen their day for sharp-shooting, military or civilian.

RIFLE SIGHTS

TELESCOPE SIGHTS

For fine work in gallery, for match shooting at two hundred yards, either off-hand or with rest, for sharpshooting with military rifles at any range, for general miscellaneous target practice about the fields and forests, for small game shooting at long range there are no other sights to compare with a telescope. For rest shooting, and I think the same could be said of military work in the prone position, there is simply no comparison between the results to be secured with good telescopic sight and any other. In off-hand work it has nearly the same superiority that it displays at rest or in the various military positions, sitting, prone, etc.

Closer holding can be done with telescope in good light than with the finest of globe and peep, or it will prove effective in light so poor that an open rear and a jack front sight can hardly be used. On the weapon of the military sharpshooter, on the Schuetzen rifle for gallery or two hundred yard range, in the humble opinion of the writer no other sight should be used. More pleasure and more game can be secured than with any other form of sight. Yet the use of telescopes in hunting or for military purposes has strict limitations.

The man who attempted to use a telescope on large and dangerous game that might take one bullet and then charge would be foolhardy. Such sight, it should be noted, practically limits the hunter to one shot, for this instrument cannot be used in snapshooting or at running game. I know that now and then some enthusiast claims the contrary, but if shots are to be taken on running game the animal would have to be moving slowly, perfectly in the open, and the time limit for firing would have to be unlimited. As to hunting, therefore, we may safely conclude that the telescope is only useful for long shots on game that we may not be able to stalk closely, like caribou, mountain goat, sheep, and African antelope which inhabit the open plain. Under such circumstances one shot directed by a 'scope may avail more than a full magazine sent with poorer aim.

However, generally speaking, a telescope is out of place on a hunting rifle. It is at best a frail instrument which cannot withstand slamming about in a boat or being jolted by a galloping horse. It renders a repeating rifle or an automatic practically nothing but a single-shot, and any time the quarry takes a notion to move, no matter if it jumps within twenty-five yards of the gun, the telescope man has a useless tool in his hands. All of which, as can readily be conjectured, quite unfits the telescope for use in the woods.

Various schemes have come forth for using a telescope in connection with open sights. Some have tried placing the open sights on top of the scope; others beneath it, or again the glass has been fitted to one side of the rifle with the usual sights in place. None of these schemes avail much. Looking under a 'scope for a snapshot, with most of the light cut off, is trying; aiming above the 'scope throws both the eye and butt of gun out of position, while trying to aim away out to one side of an unbalanced rifle is the worst of the three.

If a telescope is to be used at all on a big game rifle, it should be one of the detachable variety, to be carried at the belt except when actually needed. The mounts for the 'scope will not be found much in the way, and the glass can be put in place in a few seconds, properly aligned for some fixed distance, say three hundred yards. If the range at which the shot is to be taken doesn't coincide with the fixed elevation of the 'scope, it is easier to hold under or over with a telescope than with any other description of sight.

Telescopes for rest shooting or for sharpshooting in war should have a power of from twelve to twenty diameters; for off-hand and hunting a power of from two to eight will be satisfactory. The greater the magnification the smaller the field of view. A narrow field matters little in target shooting, but it matters much where a shot must be taken quickly at a mark which it may require time to " find " with the sight. Other things being equal, we should therefore have to sacrifice power to field of view is a hunting 'scope. However, other things are not equal, since no man can hold a glass of twenty power, in the off-hand, with enough steadiness to do good shooting.

Multiply the ordinary muzzle movements of a rifle when held in the extended arm style by twenty, and there will be such a dancing about of sight and quarry that the marksman will be willing to swear the devil is in it. Many who can use an eight power glass mounted on a heavy rifle at the range, would find a power of from two to four better adapted to game.

Some 'scopes as a means of alignment have cross-hairs, others a single hair with a ball in the middle; again they may have double cross hairs, or a pinhead after the fashion of a globe sight. Any one of these is much a matter of fancy and individual liking; the marksman, readily becoming accustomed to whichever style he prefers, will do about as good work with one as with the other.

An essential feature of the telescope is its mountings which must be strong, rigid, and precise. Where the glass is to be used on a target or military rifle, provision must also be made for micrometer elevation and windage. While a 'scope with universal focus might do for hunting a match glass must have an adjustable focus.

The majority of American telescopes are made by the Winchester Arms Company, the Stevens Arms and Tool Company, and the Malcolm Telescope Manufacturing Company. Their instruments are made of various powers for different purposes; experts declare they are splendid glasses for match and target work, also for small game shooting, but are not so good on a big game rifle owing to restricted field.

German telescopes have the greatest prestige among big game hunters. These glasses are short, easily detached for carrying in a case, have low power and large field, splendid optical qualities, a good lateral and longitudinal eye relief, but no means of securing elevation or windage. Such glasses cannot well be used on a match rifle, but on a hunting arm of high power and flat trajectory they are the best instruments cbtainable.

Comparing the American and foreign glasses, the former will do very well on a hunting rifle and nothing else equal to them is to be had for match shooting; the German is useless on the range, but superior for game. The foreign instrument costs two or three times as much as the American.

CHAPTER XVI

POSITIONS FOR RIFLE SHOOTING

THE man who is anxious to do regular skilful work on game should know something of all branches of rifle shooting. It is desirable that he be able to fire accurately from any position commonly used by a hunter, standing, kneeling, sitting, and prone. The technicalities of military shooting, such as proficiency in judging light, windage, elevation, drift, atmosphere, and humidity, will prove a beneficial knowledge. Skill in wing and snap work, too, will lead to the bagging of many a bounding deer that would otherwise escape. Two things, however, are imperative if the sportsman would be successful in killing big game, or prove a dangerous antagonist in war—a thorough foundation in off-hand firing and much practice in judging distances and conditions in shooting over unknown ranges.

163

RIFLES AND RIFLE SHOOTING

In off-hand there are several styles of holding a rifle, only one of which is really valuable to the hunter. We have off-hand with arm extended, off-hand with body rest, and off-hand with hip rest. It is well known that a target rifle shot may be a very indifferent performer on game, and while there are other reasons for this, one of the best ones is that he adopts a position that cannot be used in hunting.

Off-hand, extended arm, the common manner of holding a shotgun, is the only style in which the rifleman should train himself if his practice is to avail him in the woods and mountains. The body rest might be termed the military off-hand, many soldiers and guardsmen using it on the range. The method of aiming in the body rest is to bring the left arm in until it rests against the inflated chest, hand just in front of the guard, or the latter may be resting in the palm. In the hip-rest, the marksman takes a position that will throw out the hip upon which he rests his elbow, supporting his weapon, preferably on the tips of his fingers and thumb. The Schuetzen style of holding a rifle by means of a palm-rest is also off-hand, but Schuetzen methods are of no more use in the game field than a machine rest.

The soldier or the hunter frequently needs to place his bullet quickly, if at all; many times he must catch his quarry on the run, or it may be in view but a second or two, whereupon he must instantly throw his sights upon it and fire. Under the circumstances, posing for the body rest, or contorting for the hip-rest would be absurd.

The Schuetzen man is perfectly justified in using his position, for as a rule he makes no pretense of being a game shot, neither is he trying to develop the sort of skill available in war or sport. Nor can we blame the soldier for preferring the body rest; his officers are demanding sharpshooting results, and he must take advantage of any style of holding permitted under the rules. But when it comes to stopping a fleeing deer or a charging bear, in the words of Perlmutter, "that is something else yet," and he must shove his sights right on to the mark and let go the instant the bead covers.

Hand-holds, hip rests, hair triggers, telescope sights, heavy barrels, and miniature charges, are none of them calculated to graduate the man who must handle rapidly a light hunting rifle with a trigger pull of from three to six pounds and a kick that is sometimes hair raising. To be sure, any variety of rifle practice is better than none, but ultimately the student must be trained to the tools adapted to the work. From the foregoing it is to be taken for granted that the game shot will use the extended arm only, sticking to it persistently until he secures results.

KNEE-REST

Very often the sportsman will need to shoot from the knee. There are times when he must crawl upon his quarry in making a stalk, and he dare not rise to his feet under penalty of being seen and losing his opportunity. Moreover, the knee rest is a trifle more reliable than off-hand, quicker to learn, and steadier in a wind. In the knee rest there is plenty of give to the body and recoil is less felt than in any other position except off-hand. Where the marksman pulls deliberately or has a hard trigger it has its advantages, too, since the mark can be kept covered for a greater length of time.

The knee rest is so familiar to everybody, either from using it or seeing it used that it seems hardly worth while to describe the position. However, it means simply dropping upon the right knee and resting the elbow upon the left; the fore-end will be gripped just in front of the guard or the latter will rest in the palm. The position can be varied to some extent, and the individual will soon learn what is the easiest and steadiest for him.

SITTING

This position is used a great deal by Englishmen in target shooting with sporting rifles at one hundred yards. It is considerably more reliable than the foregoing and a great deal less practicable in the hunting field. Generally it requires so much time for the hunter to fix himself in the sitting posture that he dare not attempt it.

Some men prefer to sit down, feet placed together, knees slightly spread and an elbow on either knee, rifle pointed nearly directly to the front; others cross the legs, tailor fashion, the thighs resting securely against the sides of the feet, only the left elbow on knee, and gun swung to the left as in off-hand. The last position is the steadier and nearly as good work can be accomplished with it as in the prone.

While military authorities require that all gun

167

firing must be done free of artificial support, yet it should be borne in mind that no such restrictions apply to the hunter. He is therefore free to sit with his back resting against a tree, stump, rock, or anything else that will afford a support. Such attitude furthers the most accurate rifle firing possible in hunting. I have used it a great deal when shooting with a high power telescope and found nearly as good scores could be made as with a machine rest. The sportsman will find many opportunities to shoot in this way, as when on a stand waiting for game to approach, or when he has crawled up behind a tree he can slip about to the other side and shoot as steady as a rock. This position is quite a bit more reliable than the prone and much easier to learn.

PRONE

The prone position is that of the old-time woodsmen who were partial to resting their long barrels across a fallen tree or anything else that came handy. Some plainsmen and buffalo hunters were once in the habit of carrying a crossed stick which could be forced into the ground, thus affording a muzzle rest. However, soldiers are not allowed a muzzle rest, neither would the ballistics of a high power rifle permit it. The prone is in all respects like aiming across the log, except the barrel must be held free of support.

The finest military scores have been made in the prone, and it is the accepted position from five hundred yards up. The man who can aim and pull trigger will quickly learn to shoot in the prone and do finer work than would be possible for him in the off-hand or knee rest.

Soldiers who find it highly desirable to keep under cover will always shoot a great deal from the prone, and the hunter who is forced to crawl over bare ground in approaching game will be under the same necessity. It follows that a certain amount of practice in this position is essential to the hunter.

PRACTICING IN THE DIFFERENT POSITIONS

Rifle shooting in its final analysis is after all a very simple thing. The marksman has but to align a couple of sights with the target, hold his piece still, and pull the trigger, all very simple— apparently. However, when the novice comes to try it he discovers that he cannot stand still, or sit still, or lie still, if you place him on his back. Even with the muscles under perfect control, the heart action is disturbing, but no man that ever lived has his muscles under perfect control without continued and severe training. Not one man in ten thousand can stand still when he tries. It follows then that the first thing to be learned is to stand motionless, or sit motionless, or lie motionless, as the case may be.

Much of the preliminary training in rifle firing can be taught with an empty gun—both practice in holding and practice in trigger pulling. In the nature of things holding and trigger pulling go hand in hand, the one being useless without the other. Trigger pulling implies both nerve control, and nerve education. We will treat that subject more at length presently.

It is enough here to say that a child can pull the trigger of a gun, even when he doesn't mean to, and so can a man. But forcing the nerves of one finger to act at the exact psychological moment, not a hundredth of a second sooner or later, while every other nerve in the body remains quiescent is quite another story. The man who can do it is a rifle shot whether he can hold or not. On the other hand the fellow that can hold like a machine rest will give a good account of himself, no matter whether or not he is adept with the trigger. The marksman who combines good holding with perfect trigger pulling is a Doctor Hudson, a rare individual.

Our British cousins have proved on occasions that a green man can learn rifle shooting faster with an empty gun than when at once started in with a full charge military rifle. By way of proving to the student the value of his aiming and pulling they have invented a sub-target practice rod, a steel rod the length of the barrel, actuated by a coil spring which is released by the pull of the trigger. A target is hung up a few inches in front of the muzzle, and on pulling the point of the rod is driven into it, thus demonstrating the accuracy of the aim.

Whatever utility the sub-target rod may have, our Briton seems generally to prefer an air rifle. In air rifles there is little doubt that England leads this country or any other. Air rifle barrels are attached to the army gun, thus giving the novice the same weight, sights, and trigger pull as though he were using the service rifle. The air rifle missiles are very accurate; ten shots have been placed in a half inch circle at twenty-five yards, with power enough to drive the bullet through three-fourths inches of pine. Beyond question good practice can be had with an air gun at distances of from seven to twenty-five yards.

and ammunition is cheap, fifteen cents a thousand rounds.

In this country the .22 short takes the place of the sub-target rod and the air rifle. The ammunition is more accurate, and while it costs more, yet the man who can find time to practice will rarely consider the small cost of cartridges a matter of moment. The student with military tendencies can procure a .22 musket an army gun in all but caliber, in this way becoming perfectly familiar with the service arm. However, for general purposes the .22 single-shot or pump-action rifle will be found all sufficient.

Indoors or out, whichever may be most convenient, at distances from ten yards up the beginner should now practice at every opportunity. If his work is to be of practical benefit his off-hand firing should be with extended arm only. No desire to put up finer scores must be allowed to tempt him into trying the use of any form of hip or body rest.

When our novice tires of one position it would be well to change to another, trying the knee-rest, sitting, or prone. He will quickly discover that it is easier to put up good scores sitting or prone than kneeling or standing, and this alone should govern the bulk of his practice—the value of the work comes from accomplishing what is difficult rather than the thing that is easy.

After settling upon the best and easiest attitude, standing, kneeling, or sitting, take that position with mechanical regularity, never varying it a particle. The whole effort now is to acquire mechanical skill as indicated by trained muscles and nerves. It is not wise at this stage to attempt quick firing; the training that comes from deliberate holding is now a far better schooling.

It will shortly become evident that the knee-rest is only less difficult than the off-hand; a less number of muscles are put under strain, but these are cramped into unaccustomed positions and are certain to show the effect of it. Don't be in a hurry to finish with this preliminary practice; it is the foundation of rifle shooting skill and might well be kept up more or less persistently throughout the rifleman's life.

The object should be to make uniformly good scores rather than a few center shots and the remainder about over the target; ten shots in the bull at twenty-five yards are better than eight in a half inch and two gone wild. The regulation bull'seye at twenty-five yards is one inch in diameter. Ordinary skill would place eight out of ten shots in this when firing off-hand, as many from the knee, and ten straight either sitting or prone should not be especially difficult.

When this degree of proficiency has been reached the rifleman is ready for promotion to the outdoor brigade, ready to take up the match rifle on the range or to shoot in the woods and fields, judging distance and studying trajectories. The succeeding chapter will take up this branch of rifle firing.

CHAPTER XVII

OUT-DOOR TARGET SHOOTING

IT is to be taken for granted, now, that if the young rifleman has followed the method outlined in the previous chapter, and has practiced assiduously, he knows considerable about shooting a rifle; can at least tell when he has held a bad shot or pulled a good one. After the amount of training he has undergone he might specialize at this time, taking up the match rifle or the army gun, but if his idea is to make an all round rifle shot of himself, especially a game shot, he will do well to continue his work according to instructions given in that chapter.

Very fair target work can be secured at distances up to one hundred yards from the .22 long-rifle, provided the distance is measured or the sights are set exactly for the range, but we mean to go farther than that, shooting up to three hundred yards and farther. It follows that a new and more powerful rifle is in order.

Since the student has been accustomed to the

175

.22 caliber only, it is not wise to make too radical a change, but he should be content with a weapon that, while giving a fairly flat trajectory and good accuracy up to three hundred yards, has practically no recoil. In such a weapon we have a number of cartridges to choose from. If from motives of economy or choice the marksman prefers to reload his own cartridges, I think there is nothing better than the .25-25 Stevens. In factory loaded ammunition of higher power, however, which are really better adapted to our present purpose, either the .22 Newton H. P. or the .25-20 H. V. ought to serve every purpose.

Having our rifle, it is a foregone conclusion that we will have to get out into the woods and fields where we can use it; the man who must shoot on a measured range will have his inning later. The regulation bull'seye is two inches at fifty yards, three inches seventy-five yards, four inches, one hundred yards, six, one hundred and fifty and eight inches across at two hundred. There are finer rings inside the bull for match work, but the bull itself will do now.

Step or measure off the distance, put up a bull of a size in proportion to range with a good margin of white around it, and continue the work you have previously been doing with the .22 indoors, firing from the sitting, kneeling, standing, and prone positions.

The military and match style of rifle shooting is to change the sights every time the range varies, one elevation of back sight for one hundred yards, another for two hundred, etc., the effort being to have the sights so aligned as to strike the center whatever the distance. This is the right system of course for measured ranges, and it would be well enough to practice it for a time, marking the sight for one hundred, one hundred and fifty, two hundred, and two hundred and fifty yards.

It is well to have an assistant in this kind of work to spot the shots. Change positions frequently, firing a few shots off-hand and then sitting, kneeling, or prone, carefully noting the needed changes in elevation if any. When tired of shooting from a fixed spot, take the target from some other angle, estimate the distance, and then use the rifle to verify the judgment. The man who can keep in the eight-inch bull at two hundred yards, firing one shot standing, the next kneeling, the third sitting, fourth prone, keeping it up in rotation until ten shots have landed in the bull, has a very high order of skill so far as holding and pulling are concerned.

RIFLES AND RIFLE SHOOTING

Attempting to elevate the sights and set them for the exact range will not do for the game shooter. In the first place it frequently happens there is no time; the shot must be taken instantly when opportunity occurs. Also the system of setting sights for unknown distance is the essence of guesswork.

First we guess at the distance, next we guess at the proper elevation, then when we miss, we guess which of the previous guesses was wrong. Of course, there are times when we might note the impact of the bullet from its striking sand or water, but this happens rarely and is generally seen too late to do us any good.

In game shooting as in actual war what must be depended upon is "danger zone." The danger zone for the soldier is taken at the height of a man, sixty-eight inches, for it doesn't make any difference whether we hit him in the head or in the foot, but the danger zone for a deer is only eight inches since we must kill him outright. The problem of the game shot then is to set his sight so as to keep his bullet in this eight-inch without any further adjustment. The limits of the danger zone are about the maximum distance at which game can be killed with any certainty, and in order to strike center the rifleman must study the path of the bullet's flight or its trajectory curve, and so hold as to correct errors.

Not everything is unknown or guessed at in this case. For example, if his rifle has a four-inch trajectory at two hundred yards, he knows that it will shoot four inches high at a hundred and about two inches high at fifty or a hundred and fifty, which he must make allowance for by his holding. He cannot make this allowance, however, unless he can very closely estimate the distance and this is the present task of our rifle student.

Now is the time to begin a long and patient schooling in judging distance within sporting ranges, say up to three hundred yards. Select a variety of targets, now a knot on a tree, again a patch of moss on a bare rock. Estimate the range and hold for it. Fire several shots so as to be sure one badly held missile will not deceive you, and then go up to the target, carefully counting steps so as to verify your judgment of distance.

There are certain principles bearing on the estimation of distances which it is well to fix in the mind. On perfectly level ground with no prominent intervening objects the chances are the distance is underestimated. In rough, broken country the tendency is to overestimate. In heavy timber the probability is the range will be overestimated despite every allowance. Familiar ground will be underestimated, whereas unfamiliar lands are nearly certain to be overestimated.

The novice will shortly learn that he can hold better than he can judge the distance. A diagram of shots in an eight-inch target at some unknown distance, which he decides is about one hundred and fifty yards, is as creditable as a like target at two hundred measured yards with a spotter to mark the shots. A half dozen shots, all well held, but all missing the target owing to bad judgment of distance, will prove a lesson not easily forgotten. By and by the student will come to know both his rifle and himself, realizing that for work at unknown ranges there are well fixed limitations.

Hawks, crows, jack rabbits, wildfowl, etc., are all legitimate targets for this kind of practice. Pretty soon it will dawn upon the observant youngster that holding is not half his problem. For instance he can kill a bird the size of a hen hawk very frequently at two hundred yards if he knows the exact range, but not knowing it, his best judgment will only permit him to shoot with a good prospect of success at about one hundred and twenty-five yards. The man who can kill a crow with one bullet in three at a hundred yards (estimated) is a good shot, or a hawk at one hundred and twenty-five, or a jackrabbit at one hundred and fifty. Striking the hawk is about equivalent to hitting a four-inch, the crow a three, and the jack a six.

A hawk sitting on the dead limb of a tree with the sky for a background is a beautiful target, but hitting him at an unknown range is not so easy as it looks. I have shot at one half a dozen times, finally cutting the limb in two upon which he was sitting without touching a feather—every ball was held close enough to kill had I known the elevation.

The practice with the lightly charged, high velocity rifle should be persisted in until the marksman will be able to estimate a distance in the neighborhood of two hundred yards with such certainty that he will rarely make a mistake of greater than twenty to thirty yards whatever the circumstance of light, cover, and ground. His object is to so ground himself in this art that he can call shots fired over unknown ranges with the same certainty as the known. When he misses then he will know instantly whether it was due to a poor aim or the wrong elevation.

Half the shots which miss game and most of those that merely cripple are due to a bad estimate of the range. No man ever did or ever will judge distances perfectly when on strange ground, but the clever game shot will always be found far superior to others in this respect. Other things being equal, as shooting skill, one sportsman will still be able to take his deer with as much certainty at two hundred yards as another would at a hundred and fifty, solely because of superiority in calculating the range.

It should be remembered that the object of all this study of distance and bullet path is to enable the marksman to center his game, not land somewhere within the eight-inch. There are enough other factors tending to throw him out without wilfully permitting trajectory to do it. As an example, the hunter might fire at a deer one hundred yards away. He knows that his rifle will shoot four inches high, but does not make allowance for that knowing that the bullet will still strike within the circle. However, inadvertently he pulls the shot four inches high, and the result is a ball eight inches from center and a lost buck. On the other hand, had he aimed low, as he should, the bullet would still have proved fatal.

Having thoroughly learned to handle our rifle up to the limits of the eight-inch danger zone, it would be well now to elevate one notch, sighting to center at three hundred yards. With the Springfield '06 ammunition this would give a trajectory height of a trifle over seven inches at one hundred and fifty yards, with a .30-30 the height would be fifteen inches. Practice with this new elevation until you know it thoroughly all up and down the line. Of course the object of the three hundred yard sight is to shoot only at ranges beyond two hundred yards, but it is well to know the bullet's path both inside and beyond the distance for which it is sighted. Of course, as noted in a previous chapter, the ballistics of the rifle would govern its danger zone and when I mention sighting for two and three hundred yards, it might be taken as having reference only to rifles with a muzzle velocity of 2,500 feet or better.

DIFFICULTY OF KILLING GAME AT LONG RANGE

All of us have heard of the man who can regularly kill his game at extreme ranges. Sir Samuel

Baker tells of dropping a Cape buffalo at eight hundred yards with one ball from a muzzleloading eight bore. Another writer speaks of shooting antelope on the run at seven hundred yards, evidently a customary occurrence with him. The Boers are popularly believed to have made a common practice of shooting game at distances of from five hundred to one thousand yards. I have recently been reading of a great game shot who could strike his quarry with fair certainty at fifteen hundred yards.

Now I do not wish to maintain that such performances are impossible nor to reflect on the veracity of the narrators, but I have a suspicion that all work of this kind is sheer, bull luck, absolutely dependent on chance. With his huge, round bullet of low velocity Sir Samuel must have held a hundred feet above the buffalo's back. Shooting a running antelope at seven hundred yards requires a lead of about seventy-five feet. As for the fifteen hundred yard man it has been calculated that with our highest velocity rifle, the Springfield '06, the ball at fifteen hundred yards would be dropping one foot for every eighteen feet of forward movement consequently would fall below a twelve-inch circle in traveling nine extra feet. Estimating fifteen hundred yards to within nine feet is close work—many men could not come with-in nine feet in judging fifty.

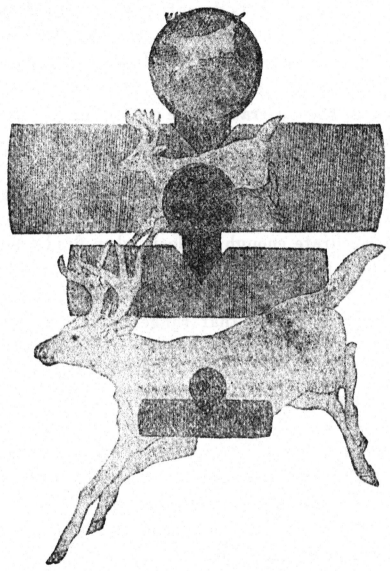

HITTING GAME AT LONG RANGE—Diagram shows front head in comparison with size of target when aiming—width of bead about the thickness of a nickel. Lower deer, 100 yds.; middle, 200 yds.; upper, 300 yds.

RIFLES AND RIFLE SHOOTING

Occasionally large game like elk and caribou have undoubtedly been killed at very long range. Our military experts do not regard a highest possible score at a thousand yards as anything wonderful, and the inference is natural that game can be shot at a like distance. However, shooting game at the moderate range of five hundred yards is not so easy as it might seem. Kindly keep in mind that, no matter what the distance, we have to land our bullet in that fatal eight-inch circle.

It is a question in the first place of having a rifle accurate enough to do it when fired from a machine rest. The Springfield is said to be our most accurate rifle, and Government tests show its mean deviation at that range to be 5.9 inches. This is not saying that all shots would go into an eleven- or twelve-inch for we have only the *average* deviation, and plenty of shots would go outside. Granted that it would stay in a fifteen-inch, that is considerably wider than an eight, and wouldn't do. The ordinary sporting rifle with soft-point bullets would require a twenty-four inch circle to contain the shots, with possibly not a single ball landing in the eight-inch.

As we see, not one of our rifles is accurate enough to shoot game at five hundreds yards. But even if they were, accuracy is not the only thing we have to consider. On the contrary when shooting over such a range we have to take into our calculation judgment of distance and correct elevation of sights, windage must not be neglected, light can by no means be overlooked, and the barometer, hygrometer, and thermometer must be read carefully; lastly we will have to get our projectile into the game with power enough to kill.

Tests by the Government show that the danger zone for infantry, with the five hundred yard alignment of sights, '06 cartridge, extends for only 128 yards back of the target. Infantry height is taken at sixty-eight inches, but our game danger zone is only eight inches across which reduces the distance to sixteen yards or thereabouts, hence if we underestimate the range sixteen yards in five hundred the result must be a miss or a crippling shot. Naturally the average game cartridge would be much inferior to the '06, an error in judging distances of more than twenty-five feet being hardly permissible.

A good stiff wind blowing across the range would easily drift a .30 caliber bullet two feet and the lightest breeze that could be felt would send it out of the eight-inch. The most moderate head wind would drop our bullet beneath the circle or if coming from the rear would drive it over the top.

Light might vary the elevation a foot or two, and the man who failed to read his thermometer would make a fatal oversight. Referring to the Government cartridge, a change in temperature from zero to 100 would increase the initial velocity one hundred and fifty feet, with a change in trajectory that would throw us wide of the eight-inch. Changes in air pressure and air moisture would do so, too, with like certainty.

From the foregoing it is to be concluded that the hunter who would kill his game at five hundred yards must have a more accurate rifle than any we now possess, must be able to estimate the distance to within a few feet, must have a wind-gauge and elevating back sight, micrometer adjusted, and must carry with him a barometer, thermometer, and hygrometer. Additionally he will have to be a mighty good shot. The average hunter is supposed to have skill enough to place half his shots in an eight-inch bull'seye at two hundred yards, and at five hundred he would do well to strike a thirty-inch with some of the bullets scattered over a five-foot circle—this wouldn't do.

However, we will say, just for the sake of argument, that the shooter could *hit* his game, how about killing it? It is generally considered that a striking energy of about 1,500 foot pounds is necessary to prove regularly effective on such game as might be shot at long range, moose for instance. Now how many rifles have this striking force at five hundred yards?

The Springfield '06 wouldn't do, having but a remaining energy of 927 foot pounds, considerably less than a .25-35 at short range, and the latter is not thought to be powerful enough even for deer. A .30-30 at five hundred yards would have no more effect on game than a .32 caliber pistol bullet. Indeed, of American cartridges I consider that the .405 Winchester is the only one that would retain sufficient energy at five hundred yards to be fairly effective on big game.

In the light of what has been said above, it is only reasonable to limit the range at which the largest game should be shot at to three hundred yards. Shots should be taken at a longer distance than this only when it is absolutely impossible to get closer, and then the rifleman is guilty of wanton cruelty to animals. Roosevelt thoroughly proved this, when in Africa, by pumping a magazine full of cartridges at a buffalo with no result other than the assurance that it would go off and die a lingering death. Van Dyke states that a deer at two hundred yards is an extremely long shot, with which I fully agree. Moreover, shooting at any game at five hundred yards is an unsportsmanlike act.

CHAPTER XVIII

A DECEPTIVE glamor lingers about the days gone by. Without reasoning the matter out, many of us have an instinctive belief that there will never be another class of riflemen like the pioneers of a hundred years ago. However, it is my belief that the real rifleman is yet to be developed, and his time will shortly be here.

I do not wish to reflect on the skill of the man with the flintlock or to insinuate that the Kentucky riflemen couldn't shoot; there is no one today who could equal their performances with the weapons they possessed, nevertheless, the strict limitations of their arms necessarily governed the ability of the men who used them. Forty-eight inch barrels as thick at the muzzle as at the breech, loaded with a small round bullet, stocked with a piece of wood that was a mere handle, and a set trigger lock, furthered nothing but deliberate work at short range.

RIFLES AND RIFLE SHOOTING

While some of these woodsmen could undoubtedly kill game in motion, since they had opportunities to practice immensely greater than any we are blessed with, yet they never took a running shot from choice. Indeed they were extremely partial to shooting from a rest whenever that was possible. Who could say that we would not do the same if we were given a rifle with an accurate range of but one hundred yards, that fizzled, flashed in the pan, and hung fire before starting its projectile on the way.

Even in the days of the Hawken rifle from 1840 to 1870, plainsmen were in the habit of carrying sticks to rest the rifle upon. Those were times when a bullet *had* to be placed right to do the work. Take it along down to within the past decade and the measure of a rifleman's skill was still his ability to bunch a series of shots, deliberately held. I believe the record for this kind of work is ten shots off-hand in a four and a half-inch circle at two hundred yards. Since the limit of accuracy in the rifle has about been reached, this is not likely to be excelled very much but even the man who can do it may not be a rifleman in the modern sense.

The twentieth century rifleman must not only shoot straight but shoot fast. His standard of excellence will not be ten shots in a four and a half inch delivered in half an hour, but ten shots in an eight-inch, all fired in ten seconds. He will kill his game as he comes to it, running, standing, and perhaps flying. It is now not beyond reason to anticipate a time when the hunter will deliberately start his deer to running in order to give it a fair sporting chance for its life, having the same contempt for a potshot that the shotgun expert has to-day.

I have spoken of this modern rifleman as "shotgun trained," not so much because he has been accustomed only to the scatter gun, as because he has developed the shotgun style of aiming to a point where it can be used with a rifle. Shotgun shooting means pulling trigger the instant our piece covers the point of aim, *never* dwelling and *never* taking a second sight, and rapid rifle fire is exactly that, no whit more and nothing less.

Our instructions heretofore have had reference to deliberate shooting, a careful and gentle manipulation of the weapon, an even and delicate pressure of the trigger, a cold control of nerve that sent the bullet on its way only when the aim is sure, time not being considered. Such work is furthered by heavy hanging barrels, set triggers, miniature loads, and " micrometer " appliances generally, but these are not for the student of rapid firing and running shooting.

The rifle for rapid firing should have shotgun weight, shotgun balance, shotgun trigger pull, shotgun fit, and the sights must be such as can be caught instantly without effort in alignment. The hands grasp the piece firmly, not with the rifleman's loose grip, but the left arm pushes forward while the right draws back, and the trigger is pulled by transferring the drawing back force to the trigger finger, and not by any conscious crooking of that finger. The moment the bead covers the mark the bullet must be under way, be the aim good or bad.

The skill in this kind of work comes, not from being able to hold the weapon as though in a vise, but to swing true to the mark, and to let-off in the hundredth part of a second, no conscious thought whatever being given to the pulling. We need not hurry our movements, indeed we can make them with mechanical regularity if we like, but just as sure as the bead rises to a certain point or swings to a certain point, the bullet *must* go.

If we hesitate, dwell, or try for a surer aim the practice is useless, and the opportunity is gone if it is running game or a disappearing target.

The training for deliberate firing is to shoot with a rifle hanging "dead," taking the utmost care not to disturb it by the pressure of the trigger. Neither does it matter how we get on the mark or how much time it takes. On the contrary rapid firing means the making of perfect *movements*. The measure of skill at a still target lies in the ability to move the sights upon it with mechanical exactness and to time the pull to the motions of the gun.

Much of the training for rapid firing can be accomplished with an empty gun; simply sight and pull trigger, keeping it up until muscles and nerves become thoroughly obedient to the will. Of course the marksman will desire to prove his progress pretty frequently by using bullets in his gun. Naturally results will depend greatly upon clever trigger pulling; sometimes the novice will let-off too soon and more often too late.

In the beginning the same accuracy must not be expected as could be secured by deliberate firing. Ten shots in a two-inch ring at twenty-five yards are pretty good. Progress, however, will generally be so rapid as to elate the rifleman highly, and in the end he may decide that he can do finer work in this style than any other.

As to the rapidity of fire, ten shots in twenty seconds is fast enough in the beginning. All this kind of work presupposes a repeating rifle, and it follows that the model of this will ultimately govern the speed with which it can be shot. With a lightly charged automatic ten shots are possible in ten seconds, all well aimed after the manner detailed; with a bolt-action gun ten shots in twenty seconds would be good, and the pump and lever would come somewhere between. Heavy hunting charges will make the marksman slower, since he must recover balance before firing again. However, this is to be said for the rapid fire system of aiming,—recoil is never felt to anything like the same extent as when the rifle is held for a deliberate aim. So true is this that most people will get their best results from light rifles, with heavy charges, when shot with the rapid fire aim.

With a hunting rifle, shot rapid-fire, it ought to be possible for the average man to place his ten shots in an eight-inch circle at one hundred yards; many can do better than this. I have seen the ten shots go into a six-inch, using a .30-30 rifle, the majority going into a four; time fifteen seconds. The man who can do this is a real game shot and a real rifleman in the modern meaning of the term.

Unquestionably the utility of quick-time firing lies in enabling us to shoot at moving objects or those that are liable to move in a deuce of a hurry. The soldier may see a rifle settling to an aim upon him and plug its owner before the latter can fire, or the hunter may catch a great buck as it tops the brush in one long leap, and would then be gone. Half the shots that a hunter wastes are thrown away because the game is running, or he is hurried out of his accustomed time for fear it will run, and the soldier of the future who cannot shoot true *and quick* will find himself in the rôle of the proverbial billet that catches the bullet.

Military authorities have arranged for rapid fire, skirmish runs, and disappearing targets. Civilian riflemen can get the disappearing target on the range by running it up out of the pit as usual and leaving it there a certain length of time. Or he can exercise his ingenuity by inventing some other kind of a disappearing target.

However, the bulk of his practice should be at a running target.

RIFLES AND RIFLE SHOOTING

It is not to be disputed that the best practice in shooting at a running target would be firing at actual game in the woods and hills, but this is not practicable unless a man lives in a country teeming with game and shoots a great deal. The ordinary sportsman who takes a yearly outing of a week or two, killing the number of bucks that the law allows, might keep it up for twenty years and know little more of shooting on the run in the end than he did in the beginning. It follows then that if he is to acquire any skill at this branch of rifle firing, he must find some artificial substitute for the living animal. Usually this takes the shape of a running deer or a running hare—a wooden or iron plate, cut into some semblance of the game it represents, and made to travel across the range on a taut wire.

A running target that can readily be constructed by an amateur and used without the assistance of a helper is made as follows: Erect two poles of such height as you wish the target to run, place them as far apart as they are high since the altitude of the poles governs the length of the run. Stretch a good stiff, straight wire between them at the desired elevation. The target itself can be made of a block of wood plated with iron, or a simple block of wood could be used if the marksman did not object to replacing

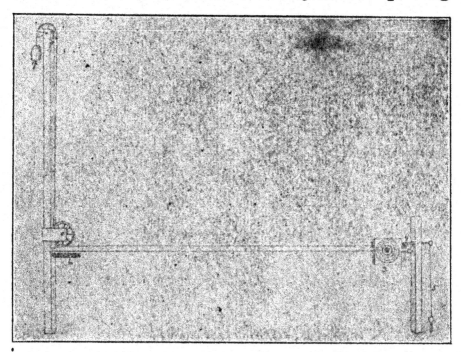

RUNNING TARGET—Tall post is 30-ft. high, posts 32-ft. apart, No. 1, pulley cord; 2, wire on which target travels; 3, target; 4, trippers; 5, trigger cord; 6, block to keep target off wheel; 7, pulley weight. Target may be made of wood or iron—iron must have a carriage.

it pretty often. Bore a hole through this block of such size that it will slip freely along the wire. Fasten a cord to the target, this cord to be run through a pulley a trifle higher than the wire, thence over the top of the pole across another pulley and down to the ground where a weight is attached. Fasten the pulling cord to the upper corners of the block so that it will be held right side up when being pulled—it might possibly be necessary to attach a weight to the bottom of the block too if it betrays a tendency to turn over when struck.

In using the target slip it along the wire from one post to the other; this will raise the weight at the end of the cord to the top of the post. Now fasten the block to the second post with a trigger or catch which will slip easily. A cord fastened to this trigger is run back to shooting position ready to release the target by jerking. When the target is released it is jerked across at the speed with which the weight falls from the top of the post.

The higher the posts the greater the speed of the target at the end of its run—friction aside it would move sixteen feet the first second and thirty-two the next. By making the poles high enough or the run long enough a speed would be attained of nearly the rate at which a bird flies. This target is only adapted to small bore rifles; large weapons would shoot it to pieces, or the necessarily thick steel would entail too much weight and friction.

By having an assistant the marksman can stand back any distance he likes until he attains a range that will force him to hold ahead from one to two feet in order to land on the target. We will go into the speed of running targets and the distance they must be led presently.

Another running target can be made by using a cash trolley carrier, exactly the kind seen in department stores. This could be operated precisely as in the store if desired, the target of heavy pasteboard being swung some distance beneath the carrier to prevent wild shots from tearing up the running gear. By starting the carrier well above the ground it will gather sufficient momentum and can be run level where shot at.

Perhaps a better scheme is to dig a trench through which the trolley wire can be stretched beneath the surface where the carrier cannot be touched by bullets. The target of cardboard is then mounted on upright wires high enough above the carrier so that it will be well exposed to view when moving. Motive power is supplied by a geared bicycle wheel with crank attached, the cord from the carrier being wound over the hollow rim of the wheel. Where clubs did not object to the expense a small gasoline engine would supply the necessary power. The carrier should have a weight swung beneath to keep the target upright. If well made and running with little friction this bicycle-power can be given a velocity of fifty feet a second, approximating the speed of a bird on the wing. Of course it can be moved as much slower as desired.

Now in shooting at a running target with a rifle we are going afoul of the same problems in lead that the shotgun has made us familiar with. To be sure a high velocity bullet has a much quicker flight than the small pellets from a shotgun, nevertheless the marksman who thinks he can center a running target by holding dead on the bull has another guess coming.

To begin with let us take up the accepted method of running shooting with a rifle. We are told in the first place not to cover and swing rapidly past the mark as with a shotgun. Such swing cannot be governed finely enough for the single missile, hence it must be at once conceded that no gain can be made on the target by the swing of our piece. On the contrary the rifleman must align his sights in front of the moving object, steadily and rather deliberately, so timing his movements that as the rifle reaches its proper elevation it will be pointed the correct distance ahead to intercept the mark.

Some point the rifle still farther ahead, stopping the weapon and holding it still while waiting for the line of sight and path of the quarry to converge. Whichever system of sighting is used, and the first is the best, it is quite evident that full allowance must be made for the time taken by the bullet in transit plus the time from the pulling of the trigger to the issue of the ball from the barrel.

Given the speed of our mark and the time of the projectile over the course it is a matter of simple calculation as to how much lead should be given in order to connect. I have had experienced hunters tell me that they simply held in front of a fleeing buck, pulling as the sights "filled;" on the other hand Van Dyke speaks of holding an entire jump ahead of a deer and centering him. We will see who is right. These calculations are made for an animal running at right angles to the line of fire, which of course he might not do, and if moving off at a gentle angle the "sight filling" would be all right.

Take our highest velocity rifle, the '06 Government, and the time of the bullet's flight over a 200 yard course is .244 of a second. Add to this one-fiftieth of a second, the average time for pulling trigger, action of lock, and bullet through the barrel, and we have .264 of a second as the elapsed time from our mental calculation to the landing of the bullet. Remembering that a man can run thirty feet in a second we will have to grant a deer a speed of at least forty feet. Now admitting that the beast is moving at that rate, he would cover ten feet while the bullet was reaching him, or with the slower .30-30 bullet fourteen feet. Van Dyke shot a much lower velocity projectile than either of these, and no doubt he was perfectly correct in estimating a lead of sixteen to twenty feet for a running deer at two hundred yards.

A race horse can run a mile in one minute and forty seconds or a little better than that. This means fifty-three feet a second, and while I think the race horse the fastest animal living, yet I believe that an antelope would cover fifty per second, which at a range of four hundred yards would carry him twenty-eight feet while the bullet was traveling to him. We can thus see that shooting running antelope at a quarter of a mile is not so easy as some people would have us believe.

Of course deer and other animals sometimes run at a gentle canter, but even a man walking across the range at four miles an hour at a distance of two hundred yards, would be missed if we held square upon him. Considerations which may be inferred from the above reduce the range at which running game can be killed with any certainty to one hundred yards, or a trifle over. In my experience I have never seen but one deer killed running at over two hundred yards, and then there were four moving single file, head to tail, and I doubt if the marksman knew which he held upon.

Coming down to our artificial running target, and shooting at the accepted range for this work, 100 yards, when the mark is traveling at the rate of 10 feet per second the lead should be 1.16 feet; 20 feet per second, 2.32; 30 feet per second, 3.48; 40 feet per second, 4.64; 50 feet per second, 5.80; 60 feet per second, 9.96. These calculations are made for the Government rifle with a muzzle velocity of 2,700 feet; ordinary sporting weapons would require considerable more allowance. Moreover if a man were slow on the trigger or dwelt on his aim the Lord knows how far ahead he would have to hold. These figures are for the fiftieth of a second for pulling and time out of the barrel, and that is pretty fast.

The English style of running deer shooting is to fire two shots, a right and left, while the mark is traveling about sixty feet, at thirty feet a second. The number of shots we might fire would naturally be limited by the velocity of the mark. The character of weapon we used would have its influence, too. At the given rate of speed and distance under fire, an automatic ought to get in three shots, a lever-action rifle two, but I doubt if the average rifleman with a bolt gun could do better than fire the one shot.

This is not a treatise on deer shooting, yet a word on the subject. A buck at full speed, especially when first sprung, bounds high. It will not do to attempt to hit him while he is rising or even at the height of his leap; hold low and in front, about where he will alight, for he always seems to remain at this point for the greatest length of time. Even when the animal is running straight away hold rather low—his apparent line of "flight" invariably appears to be higher than it really is, what impresses the eye being the top of his bounds where he is in plainest view.

CHAPTER XIX

WINGSHOOTING with a rifle of the kind rendered familiar by the professional trick and fancy shots is a very entertaining recreation. Moreover, such work is of considerable utility; the man who can burst a walnut tossed up at forty feet is very apt, within reasonable range, to double up a bounding deer.

This description of rifle shooting is much the most sensational of all rifle work, with practice feats being accomplished that border on the marvelous. It is, too, I believe the easiest branch of rifle firing in which to develop skill, since anyone who is expert in the use of a shotgun will make very rapid progress in the game of fancy snapshooting with a rifle. Many become proficient in this style who could never make a great reputation in the more legitimate lines of rifle firing. Nevertheless, many of our professional snapshots, like the Topperweins, practice long

207

and faithfully, their rifle shooting ability, though guided in a different channel, not being second to that of our greatest military and match shots.

The so called "champion" rifle shots, who proclaim themselves such from having broken the greatest number of glass balls in a thousand or fifteen thousand, do not deserve much credit except for endurance. Striking a three-inch disc at fifteen feet is not a wonderful performance. Maurice Thompson demonstrated that he could do it with a bow and arrow, getting forty-four out of fifty his first public attempt. I believe the fifteen foot, three inch record is fifteen thousand straight, which alone should tell the story. However, the snapshot who is in earnest about acquiring actual and practical skill need not confine himself to three-inch blocks tossed straight up at fifteen feet.

The choice of rifle cartridge for snap shooting should lie between the .22 short, .22 long-rifle and .22 automatic—the .22 short is good enough, but the automatic would have to be used by those who preferred a self-loading gun. Cartridge economy is worth considering now because snap-shooting eats up ammunition with an insatiable appetite. The rifle ought to be light, well balanced, with a fitted stock, in model either a pump-action or an automatic; the latter is the fastest, but the other is fast enough and has the better trigger pull. Of course a single-shot would do for wingshooting, but the ambitious student will soon reach a point where the firing of one shot at an object will not content, but he must get off two or three ere his mark strikes the ground.

In sights, some profess to be able to use the tang peep with large aperture, but all professionals prefer open sights of a rather coarse description, large bead front and wide notch in the rear. The Lyman jack sight is a good bead or the Sheard, with a slightly crescent shaped rear bar. Align the sights to shoot center at fifty feet when the full front bead is taken, no effort being made to draw the bead fine, since that is impossible in snapshooting.

Let the trigger pull be quick and sharp without the least perceptible drag or any irregularity whatever; the customary weight of pull on the shotgun is about right, yielding with a pressure of three to four pounds. The automatic has a heavier pull than this which prevents the rifle from being acceptable to many, though others do good work with it.

Having the rifle, the next thing is to practice with it, everlastingly practice. The ordinary rifle wingshot will fire a hundred rounds a day to begin with and may presently find himself using a thousand.

Begin at the beginning, that is with the easiest possible feats. Throw up empty quart cans (the assistant does this) straight into the air ten feet high and ten feet distant from the gun. Almost any ten year old boy can begin to hit these after a few attempts, but if the cans prove to be too small try an old tin pan. Success will beget success in this game in very short order.

When the cans can be struck with considerable regularity at ten feet, increase the range a few feet at a time until they are being tossed up at a distance of thirty feet from the gun. With the longer range, it should be noted, the targets are to be thrown up a trifle higher. Keep up the work with the cans until nine out of ten and ten hits straight are frequent; then blocks of wood can be substituted for the tins, but have large blocks at first, not less than four inches in diameter, and when changing to the smaller targets go back to the shortest range again and run through the list of objects.

The original practice should now be repeated with the blocks, gradually increasing the range to thirty feet. With gaining skill reduce the size of the mark, but be satisfied with reasonable progress—early attempts to duplicate the work of a professional are very discouraging, and it should never be forgotten that they learned the A, B, Cs before they could read. By and by, the targets being thrown straight up at a moderate distance, the marksman should find little difficulty in striking an object the size of a walnut with great regularity.

In this work one important thing may have been noted by the shooter, he doesn't swing on his target and shoot with a moving barrel as he would with a shotgun, but throws his sights beneath the moving mark where he stops his piece until the falling target cuts the line of sight, when he pulls. The difficulty of the game is not so much holding the rifle as gauging his pull so that the trigger will yield exactly as the descending target cuts the line of sight. Where the marksman is slow on trigger he may have to pull just under, while if quick and sensitive of nerve the shot can be directed at the lower edge of the mark. The real allowance at thirty feet is not so much for the speed with which the block is falling as it is the time required for putting thought into action in pressing the trigger. In the matter of acquiring instantaneous nerve response to the will the snapshot is superior to any other class of marksmen.

The principle of snapshooting with a rifle is to fire with a still arm only, the target alone moving. If the rifle and target are both moving, the problem becomes much more complex, indeed practically impossible with difficult shots. It follows that no great amount of lead can be given in fancy rifle shooting, but the marksman must catch his target when it is moving slowly, as when just beginning its descent, and the range must not be so great that much consideration will be required for the bullet's time to the mark, or for the space covered by the latter in the interim. Not one fancy shot in a hundred could strike a six-inch disc tossed up at fifty yards, which shows us the strict limitations of the game.

Nevertheless the amateur who is desirous of acquiring practical skill should not stop where many of the professionals do, that is with targets thrown with great uniformity at a stipulated distance, but having acquired the knack of placing his bullets upon the mark when it is tossed straight up, it is now time to vary the flight. Have the assistant begin throwing the blocks across the gun from right to left. Misses will surely follow for a time, but by and by the marksman will begin to learn the new curve of flight, getting his rifle in front of the mark on its exact line of movement, when he can do this regularly it is only a matter of gauging the time to pull as before.

Now other angles of flight can be tried, as from left to right, incomers, or the helper can stand beside the marksman throwing the block straight away. As noted previously a point will always be found where the target is moving slowly while descending to cut the line of aim. I might say here that I have never yet seen a man who could do much with the target while it was rising. Such work would be contrary to the principle of the game, shooting with a still barrel, also fatal to the trick and knack of it.

When beginning practice with a new line of flight, it will generally be wise to return to the large target like the tin can, but the smaller blocks can soon be substituted again. The smaller the object shot at the greater the skill required to strike it, of course, and the man who can regularly hit a marble tossed up at forty feet is a dandy. Indeed, execpt for the sensation of the thing it is never worth while to shoot at objects so small that they would be difficult to hit if at rest. Rather ground yourself on variety of flights, the target being of moderate size, say two inches, and increase your distance from the mark as much as your skill will possibly admit. The longer the distance at which the mark can be struck, in the greatest variety of flights, the more beneficial the practice to either the shotgun shooter or the rifleman.

Having become expert at the tossed up targets, firing but the one shot at them, doubles might now be attempted, especially if the student is anxious to shine as an exhibition shot. Naturally for the doubles and triples speed must be developed. Rapid aiming not only for the first bullet but those following, would entail some sacrifice of accuracy, so return to the tin can again. When it can be struck from three to five times before it falls, replace with the smaller blocks as usual. The beginning of the rapid repeat work should be with the targets thrown straight up, afterwards all the various angles can be learned. I need hardly mention that the nearer the target gets to the ground, or the farther it has fallen, the more allowance must be made for its speed of movement, but the manner of holding is always the same—align the sights under and shoot with a still gun.

Bursting bricks and then the pieces, striking

coins, bullets, etc., is merely a matter of long and hard training. It really seems that the crack fancy rifle shot can hit an object in the air about as readily as he could at rest. Very few of them, however, are able to make any practical use of their acquirements when it comes to game shooting.

Many would conclude that the men who can hit a bullet in the air would surely stop a wild duck or a quail, yet I have never heard of anyone who even claimed he could do it with any certainty. The secret of their failure in game shooting lies in the fact that their customary tossed-up target is governed by fixed laws, except as its flight may be disturbed by the wind, while the flight of the bird is controlled by its own will and none can foresee what it will do the next instant. At best very few birds fly in a straight line with unvarying speed which would have to be the case if they were to be killed with a rifle.

However, we will now continue our snapshooting practice beyond the point where trick shots stop with the direct idea of developing a skill that may assist us in shooting running or even flying game. Take a dart some five feet in length, with a head two inches broad, and a shank four inches across and eight long, and have it thrown by hand, Greek fashion, past the marksman at a distance from him of thirty or forty feet. The rifleman can attempt to place his shot either upon the head or the shank and with practice will be able to accomplish the feat. He can augment the speed of the dart, too, if he likes, by having it sent by means of a throwing stick and cord, until it is traveling at such a rate that he will have to make a two-foot lead at twenty yards.

Having graduated with the dart, our expert can take up clay bird shooting with a rifle. It will soon become evident to him that he cannot hit straightaway birds, sent at ordinary speed, and the strength of the trap will have to be reduced. Then instead of standing behind the trap as does the shotgun man, he should go out into the field and try the targets as they go past him at lessened velocity. After a little practice he will be able to hit some of them, though I have never yet seen a man who could break any great percentage—one in three would be excellent shooting.

Fair overhead birds, sent at a height of about twenty-five feet, can be struck with considerable certainty, shooting shotgun style, covering the bird, barely hiding it by the barrel and firing. This is hardly rifle work, though, since all the shooting should be accomplished on the system outlined in the beginning, throwing the rifle in front of the line of flight, steadying it, and pulling as the flying object cuts the aim. As previously noted, swinging shooting will not do with a rifle; even when the mark is as large as a deer, the swing will generally prove a failure.

The post-graduate course for the fancy rifle shot is shooting game. A running squirrel, or a cottontail is a fair mark upon which to test skill— in fact so far as the squirrel and the cottontail are concerned, I believe it is the only sportsmanlike method of killing them. Neither has much chance for its life in front of a shotgun, and little more when sitting before a rifle. Let bunny be bounding down a corn row, though, or circling through the trees, and he who trips him up with a small bore rifle has done something worth remembering. A squirrel, too, is a beautiful mark as he runs to the end of a limb where he pauses to make his leap just long enough to permit a lightning snapshot, then jumps, catches another limb, and hangs while the marksman pumps in another. Again he glides along a limb, barely showing the top of his back, while the gunner send splinters and bark flying before, behind, and under him, finally landing a bullet home.

For this work I would advise a heavier cartridge than the .22 short which will not kill half of the time it hits, especially with a tenacious little beast like a squirrel. The .22-11 rimfire is a good cartridge for this work, though I think the .25-20 is better. It should be borne in mind that no such quantities of ammunition will be used in game shooting as have been devoted to the tossed up targets.

Quail and wild ducks are not entirely beyond the skill of the rifle snapshot. I have known a man to kill five quail in the course of a day, all shot fairly on the wing with a rifle. He was only successful with one style of flight, a bird that rose close to the gun and bore away, not straight, but at any easy angle. He then shot in the usual way by throwing his sights in front and pulling just before the game covered them. Any shot in which an allowance of more than a couple of inches had to be given was nearly sure to result in a miss and straightaway birds were rarely hit. The wildfowl that I have seen killed were rising birds, angling gently off, and never passing ducks, however close they might come. Snapshooting game with a rifle is withal a fascinating pastime, one bird so killed affording more satisfaction than several dropped before a shotgun.

SNAP AND WINGSHOOTING

Prairie chickens can be killed on the wing with a rifle, where they are plentiful and tame, especially the sort of immature birds that used to be shot in August. I have been told that a professional trick shot, on a wager, once hit seven swallows in a hundred shots, but I didn't see it done. John Winston, the live pigeon shot, used to go quail shooting with a rifle occasionally, bringing back bags of birds which he said were all killed on the wing—I never happened to be out with him. Yet I think it is within the skill of man to kill an occasional bird of any kind on the wing with a rifle, quail, chicken, wild goose, duck, crow, or hawk.

The finest work I have ever heard of was described by Stonehenge, the English sporting writer, who tells of a British gamekeeper who killed fifty live pigeons in a hundred shots, fifteen yards rise, muzzleloading rifle. Nevertheless, when all is said, the man who would do his wingshooting with a rifle must possess a deal of patience and fortitude. What anyone can do though is vastly to improve the accuracy of his wingshooting with a shotgun and his chances at big game with a large bore rifle.

The professional shot's stock in trade, such as firing while standing on his head, bending over backwards, aiming with rifle upside down, aiming by means of a mirror, etc., are all silly and not to be imitated by a selfrespecting amateur.

CHAPTER XX.

TWO HUNDRED YARD SHARPSHOOTING

TWO hundred yard sharpshooting is one of the finest recreations connected with the use of a rifle, or for what matter any other tool. Our present off-hand sharpshooter combines the ethics of the old long rifleman of a former century with the ideals of the German or Swiss Schuetzenman.

The typical American rifleman of the past was a grim and quiet chap who shot close and said nothing; he had a deadly concentration that made him unrivaled in war, but he didn't know how to play. The Schuetzenman loved the sport for its own sake. He took his family with him to the shooting park; he ate much, drank some, talked a plenty, laughed long and loud, and shot a heap whether he hit or not. Of the two classes, one was the better shot, the other the better sportsman.

Formerly the German and the American shot at

different targets, on separate ranges. The native son used the Standard target, a freak offspring of the military, while the Schuetzenman had his own German ring target, man target, point target, and eagle target. The American would have preferred " string measure," an exact value for every shot, had that been practicable, while the German was a great lover of chance and luck with a partiality for the eagle target in which a wooden bird was shot to pieces, the man fortunate enough to strike a certain piece being crowned " King." He liked the man target, too, with its vertical lines in which a shot ten inches off might count as much as a dead center. The American's standard of excellence was a long series of shots without a wild thrown bullet; the German gave his prize to the one who landed a single bullet in the center. One style of shooting eliminated the mediocre, the other encouraged the novice.

The arms used differed widely, too, at one time. The German clung to his great Schuetzen rifle with its hair trigger, set so light that an Irishman could start it with a cuss word, though it didn't mind a Dutch oath. Besides he would tolerate no rule that barred his palm-rest, and long, heavy barrel; neither could be see more merit in the standard target than in his own Ring—in which at least he was right. On the contrary the American usually shot under the rules of the Massachusetts Rifle Association which forbade palm-rests, rifles of over ten pounds weight, or triggers with a minimum pull of less than three pounds. The idea of one rifleman was ultimately to use his skill in hunting and war, the other shot purely for sport and the making of record scores.

Gradually, through a process of evolution and elimination, the two classes have come together in the present generation. The German still uses his " lucky " targets, but no longer values very highly the records made upon them, while the American has discarded his ten pound, three pound pull gun for the Schuetzen rifle, recognizing the utility of the German appliances, palmrests, set triggers, Schuetzen butt plates, cheek pieces, and has gone him one better by inventing muzzleloading barrels and insisting upon telescopic sights.

The old Schuetzenman, born across the water, loved his brass band, his marching and countermarching, his ribbons and decorations, his beer, and his much shoot and little hit. Not so his son who will be found in the quietest corner of the shooting stand, saying nothing and sawing wood, the finest off-hand sharpshooter in all the world. On the other hand the American youth has deserted his own ranges and gone to the German mostly because he appreciates the need of a social side to the game; the jollity and wholesome fun of the Schuetzenfest appeal to him. The result is a new generation of rifleman who shoot together in all amity and whose work is far superior to anything seen in the past.

Whatever the practical value to the hunter or the soldier of practicing sharpshooting under modern conditions, and I do not credit it with having much, the sport itself is worthy of all praise. Moreover as a training in self control, controlled muscles, and nerve education it is superior to any sport in the world.

The man who would participate in off-hand match shooting must first of all look to his rifle. The ordinary military, the sporting, or hunter's weapon is quite useless. He must select a Schuetzen rifle and prepare to manipulate it Schuetzen fashion.

The most advanced type of the Schuetzen rifle is shown in cut published herewith. It has much to recommend it, yet a visit to the range will show that nearly every expert has modified and changed it to suit his own notions. Since, however, it would be impossible to describe at

length all the variations that personal requirements demand I shall content myself by pointing
out the features of the rifle illustrated which might
be termed peculiarly Schuetzen.

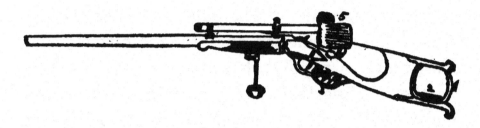

MODEL OF SCHUETZEN RIFLE—1. Butt-plate with shoulder
support. 2. Plate, 2-ins. wide, to support arm. 3. Lever
with block of wood grooved for each finger. 4. Thumb-hole
to prevent thumb from being strained away from fingers.
5. Blinder.

The barrel is the Pope-Stevens with bullet
seated from the muzzle as described under heading
of Match Ammunition, Chapter VIII. The most
desirable caliber is there mentioned also.

The sight should be the best telescopic match
glass procurable, power from four to eight,
micrometer adjusted for windage and elevation
so as to give an inch to the line at two hundred
yards. Whatever might have been true in the
past, it is to-day impossible to compete successfully with peep and globe sights. Ignore spirit
levels; the contrivance is useless in off-hand shooting.

PALM-REST

The palm-rest is the Winchester, and is adjustable for length and angle without the use of tools; some prefer it fixed more toward the frame and others forward. The palm-rest is something that American riflemen once fought bitterly and consistently, rigidly barring it from their matches. Nevertheless they beat the devil around a stump by getting the effect of the palm-rest through balancing the rifle on the end of the thumb and the finger tips—some marksmen shoot in that position yet. This manner of holding is hard on the fingers when the piece is heavy, and otherwise is inferior to the handhold.

The palm-rest serves the double object of permitting the elbow to rest on the hip without unduly contorting the body, also preventing the hand from gripping the barrel which is inimical to evenness of elevation. It is difficult to grip a barrel with exactly the same force every time; the clasp of the hand may tighten or loosen and the contracting fingers of one hand have an effect on the other, causing irregularity of trigger pulling. All this, it might be noted, applies equally to other rifles as well as the Schuetzen, but a degree of accuracy which would be considered satisfactory with a hunting weapon would not rate as third class work with the match rifle. Delicately set Schuetzen triggers can only be used advantageously where the rifle is balanced rather than held, either on the finger tips or palm-rest.

The palm-rest is now in general use by American and German riflemen alike. The man who possessed none would be badly handicapped in a long series of shots, whatever his skill might be. It is not a handsome contrivance, but of its utility, there can be no question; rifles weighing above fifteen pounds could hardly be shot effectively without it.

CHEEKPIECE FOR TELESCOPE

The cheekpiece is also the Winchester; cut with especially high comb to adapt it to a telescope which is placed a full inch higher above the barrel than ordinary sights. It follows that where a glass is mounted an ordinary low comb and check will be practically useless padded up to the required height. A drop of an inch at comb will generally be found sufficient, but the slant to butt must be rapid, down to at least three inches; some prefer four. The cheekpiece, together with the blinder, affords a very secure rest for the head, and on its perfect fit largely depends the ease and security with which the rifleman holds his gun.

THE BLINDER

Generally speaking, the advice to shoot a rifle with both eyes open the same as when firing a shotgun is good. It applies especially, though, to game shooting, rapid firing, and where distance must be estimated at the time of taking aim. With the long, deliberate aim of the match shooter it has been found trying to concentrate the brain's attention entirely upon what the sighting eye sees when both are open. On the other hand squinting one eye hurts the vision of the other, and this will not do. Hence we have the blinder.

This is a piece of moderately thick sole leather, fitted to the end of the 'scope, then bent and shaped to curve around the head over the left eye. The blinder has three distinct purposes. It covers the left eye, obviating any necessity for squinting it, at the same time shutting off all side light either from the right or the left. It is fitted over the end of the 'scope in such a manner as to act as a guard, preventing injury to the eye from recoil, and the heavy leather is an elegant head rest, firmly locking the head to the gun. As riflemen put it, a shooter crawls into his blinder and goes to sleep only to wake up with the crack of the gun and the marker signaling a 25.

THE SCHUETZEN LEVER

The Schuetzen lever is made in many styles with almost as many variations as there are individual marksmen. The author has designed one which he has found more satisfactory than anything at present furnished by the factories. The object of this lever is to place the fingers in such position that the forefinger will exert its pressure directly to the rear without any strain or tendency to press upward toward the thumb. Each finger has its own grooved rest in which it simply lies in a natural bend without any forced contraction or grip, which might involuntarily extend to the pulling finger, causing a premature let-off. When the fingers grip the stock, as in an ordinary rifle, it is almost impossible to manipulate the sensitive double trigger without an occasional accidental pull.

The spur lever is better than a pistol grip, but the middle finger which curves around it has a natural tendency to contract further until the tip of the finger rests on something; nothing is there to afford this rest and the consequent strain is communicated to the pulling finger. The whole idea of the "block lever" with finger grooves is to have the hand in a rest so natural and secure that the forefinger can lie against the most sensitive trigger without the marksman having a particle of fear of an involuntary pull, yet the finger will respond instantly to the will of the marksman.

Since half of off-hand shooting lies in correct trigger pulling, it follows that every contributing feature, including the triggers themselves, must be studied carefully. It is a universal complaint among riflemen that while they can hold well enough they cannot let-off. If a man could discharge his weapon by will power alone, our present rifle records would be discounted in a jiffy.

Fairly good double set triggers are furnished by the factories, but an expert gunsmith who makes a specialty of that sort of thing can improve them greatly. They should be adjusted to a very light pull, the greater the skill of the marksman the more delicate trigger he can handle. However, the trigger must never be so sensitive that it cannot be touched at all without yielding. I have seen more than one novice afraid of his trigger, making a little dab at it when ready to fire—needless to say he couldn't shoot. The finest double set triggers that I have ever seen were those made by William Bauer of the Central Sharpshooters' Association, St. Louis. No movement was perceptible to the eye when these triggers yielded to pressure.

THUMB REST

A peculiar feature of the typical Schuetzen rifle is the thumb rest. Where to place the thumb when firing a rifle is always a problem. If placed on top of the tang it spreads the hand too much, causing an upward contraction of the forefinger in place of to the rear. To such an extent is this true that sometimes two ounces of force are necessary to pull the trigger where one ought to suffice. For this reason some place the thumb along the side of the grip in place of over it, but then it has nothing to rest upon. The problem has been solved by cutting a groove into the grip the size of the thumb, over which extends a steel plate. In this groove the thumb rests as securely as the fingers do in their place on the lever.

THE SCHUETZEN BUTT-PLATE

The butt-plates that come on factory rifles

have a variety of shapes, but those manufactured by private individuals differ still more. The Schuetzen rifle is not held like an ordinary weapon but is balanced. Without the Schuetzen butt there would be a tendency for it to lift away from the shoulder, a tendency that would have to be counteracted by a grip and rearward pressure—something to be avoided. Exacting riflemen have usually had butt-plates made to order, many having the lower arm long and upcurved back of the shoulder.

In off-hand rifle shooting with extended arm the right elbow is held rather high and would be under considerable strain if the aim were continued for any length of time. In deliberate Schuetzen work the arm is dropped until it rests against the butt, this both to hold the rifle in balance and to relieve the arm muscles of all unnecessary labor.

The most nearly perfect arm and shoulder support made is cast from solid brass, the back plate an inch and a half in width, broadening under the arm to two inches. This sort of butt-plate will so lock a man to his gun that a fifteen pound rifle will balance as though it had grown to him.

With a rifle of the sort described here, holding is simplified to training the leg muscles to support the body, second after second, without an iota of movement; to regulating the breathing, and to so distending the chest that the heart beating will not communicate its action to the rifle. Probably the leg training is the most difficult, and the majority would be able to hold steadier if permitted to place the left leg against a solid support.

SHARPSHOOTING

Having our rifle, it only remains to practice—continual, never-ending, patient, persistent, studied practice. It is true that some men of strong nerves, good physique, and keen eyesight can develop rifle shooting skill more quickly than others, but it is no less true that the man who has made the greatest reputation as a sharpshooter is he who has worked the hardest for it. There is absolutely no exception to this and no royal road leads anywhere near success.

Probably the best scheme for the rifleman living in the city is to have two barrels for the rifle, one a .22 for the gallery and the other of larger bore for the range. Except in the matter of judging wind and light, gallery practice is almost as valuable as shooting the full distance. A certain number of shots should be fired daily, say with the .22 ten strings of ten shots to the score, all pulled with the utmost care. During his match shooting days the writer had a range of his own and made it a rule in good weather and bad to fire fifty shots every day at two hundred yards.

Take care to handle the rifle with machine-like, mechanical regularity. Place the feet exactly so every time, wear the same amount of clothing, fit the butt to its precise place on the shoulder, stand long enough to quiet the nerves and heart action, take a long breath or two, like a diver preparing to go under, and then settle the rifle to its aim. Find your steadiest method of swinging onto the bull and use that exclusively. Generally the rifle shots will be aligned above the bull, then the weight of the piece will settle it firmly into place, to swing gently back and forth across the target.

Along with muscle training will have to come nerve education. The great problem of rifle shooting is unity of action between brain and trigger finger. The student will soon discover that he can hold and hold, perhaps keeping the sights on the dead center for seconds at a time; he will pull and pull, but the trigger will not yield, though he knows a pressure of an ounce or two would start it. Of a sudden his sights begin to move off the mark and he tries to ease up on the trigger, when bang goes the gun—wild shot, of course.

What was he doing all the time he thought himself putting ample pressure on the trigger? He cannot tell, nor can anyone else more than conjecture. Perhaps he was really pressing the trigger but not quite hard enough; possibly he was pulling with the whole hand except the trigger finger, exerting all the force on the grip of the rifle; more likely he was not putting a grain of weight on the trigger, though *his brain distinctly told him that he was.* His " motor " nerves were locked rigidly by the effort of holding the rifle still, but the moment the piece moved the brakes were off and so was the shot.

The man who can pull trigger while his gun is hanging as though in a vise can shoot like a machine, but such an individual I have never seen. The shot must be pulled within the fraction of a second after the bead settles to the center or on go the " control brakes " and he will have to let the rifle move off to try again. No matter how well the shooter is holding, if he keeps on pressing after the trigger has refused to move at the dictate of his will, the first thing that *must* happen is the release of the nerves which control steadiness, and the rifle is bound to move before the trigger can be pulled.

Individuals differ, and the writer can best give his personal experience. In my shooting the pressure on the trigger was started just an instant before the sight covered the center, with the expectation that the trigger would yield at the precise time when the rifle settled " dead " in the middle of the bull. If my anticipations were realized I got a shot in the 24; if the trigger let go too soon, most likely the shot was as good as a 22, but if the trigger failed to release the lock on time, and getting impatient I *forced* the pulling to get value for a fine hold, the shot could not be called accurately and might go out of the bull. When anxious to make a fine score I never forced, but trying about three times for a perfectly timed let-off and failing, would then take the rifle down from the shoulder and rest.

I believe this is the common experience of trained sharpshooters, and the patience and forbearance with which they will try again and again for a pull-off is something remarkable. Naturally such extreme care would only be used in the last rounds of a good score when one badly held shot would render futile all the good ones preceding.

SHARPSHOOTING

By way of proving this point and at the risk of being thought egotistical, I shall have to describe an incident of my own work. When shooting at the tournament of the Central Sharpshooter's Association at St. Louis I had scored on the German Ring Target 24, 23, 23, and had one shot to fire. H. M. Pope, of Hartford, Conn., had already made 94 in his four shots, and in order to tie him I had to make a 24 while a 25 would win. For thirty minutes I tried to get a perfect pull, going back to the stand again and again before I got it, a 24 which tied for first. The man who won third, H. D. Schneidewind, of Belleville, Ills., told me that he spent an hour and a half pulling his last shot, but he finally got his 24.

Such extreme care as this is liable to defeat itself, through an accidental let-off or one of the many things that can happen and spoil a good score. With rifles cracking to right and left, and impatient marksmen behind awaiting their turn, witholding fire for a perfect pull is a nerve-racking business, but such is sharpshooting at a national tournament.

As in other rifle shooting a great deal of the training for holding and pulling can be accomplished at home in the room or yard without the use of ammunition. Put up a bull's eye corresponding in size according to distance with the regulation bull. Place an empty shell in the gun and sight on this bull and pull, and keep it up until thoroughly tired—train in this way every day, as often as time permits.

In this way the rifleman can so train his muscles that his sights will never quite move off the bull in the wildest movement they make while he is trying to pull. Only when he can hold continually on the black for seconds at a time can he consider himself a reliable shot, for it is to be expected that occasionally a shot will go when the sights are at their widest swing and if this is outside the bull, some of the bullets will miss it before a hundred are fired. The acme of skill is never to let a shot go outside the bull, and never let the sights swing out after the finger settles to the trigger.

The manner of bringing the sights onto the center is something for the individual rifleman to solve in his own way. The proverbial instruction is for the marksman to bring his piece up from beneath until the sights cover the bull and then press trigger. This will not do with a heavy Schuetzen rifle balanced on a palm-rest.

The tendency of the big weapon is to swing across the bull horizontally, back and forth.

SHARPSHOOTING

Some men of quick nerve action can pull as the rifle swings, without altogether stopping it, and get good results. Usually they press the trigger while the piece is moving from right to left since the rifle in its left swing hardens and sets the muscles, consequently traveling more slowly. Probably a better system of regulating the swing is to have the left extremity of the movement just reach the center where the weapon must "hang" for an instant before beginning the return to the right side.

In my case I found that my rifle had a pretty regular swing but not pendulum like. It moved off the center to the right, rose a trifle, and then settled down across the bull from two o'clock to six, where I endeavored to stop it and let off— failing to get the pull it would again move off to the right and around as before. If I was in my best form, and using telescope, the sight would never quite leave the twelve-inch. All my premature shots would be to the right and high, delayed let-offs low, and now and then the rifle jumped beyond control throwing the ball high and to the left. In sharpshooting it is a great and fascinating gamble as to what is going to happen when the marksman settles his rifle on the black, but when the perfect pulls come regularly he has a feeling of power the nearest to omnipotent ever vouch-safed to man.

After a little experience on the range the rifle-man can begin calling his shots, telling where they went before the marker signals. The more expert the shooter the closer he can call. It is nothing uncommon for a skilled shot to " call " his bullet within an inch of where it has gone. To do this he must not only see where the sights were when he pulled, but must keep his eye on them and note where they jumped to with the recoil. If the rifle rises straight across the bull with its recoil the marksman can expect to find his bullet where he sighted it, but if it jumps out badly to either side expect a bad shot in that direction. It is much easier to call shots with a lightly charged, heavy barreled rifle than with one much influenced by recoil.

It will not do to strain the eye too much in sighting. Experience will teach the shooter that the greatest clearness of vision lasts for but a short time, and then it fades to return again—this happening in regular rotation. The pull-off must then be so timed as to take place when the vision is the clearest, if the shot is to be called acurately.

The training of muscle and nerve is as arduous

in a crack rifleman as that of the finest juggler in the world—in fact of all human beings he has the most perfect muscle control. Not only from seeing, but from feeling and mental calculation he has the most delicate perception of the movements of his piece. To such stage of perfection is the training in *feeling* where his rifle is pointed carried that after placing it upon the bull he can tell exactly the spot his sights are covering without again looking at them. I have known a marksman to sight his rifle, then shut his eyes, pull the trigger to order, and get a bulls'eye—sometimes. While holding and not looking, of course, he had a mental picture of where the sights were swinging every instant of the time.

A word on wind and light. An even wind blowing across the range and not too strong permits almost as fine shooting as a calm. However, when it has sufficient force to carry the ball quite out of the bull with windgauge at zero very fine scores should not be expected, but the marksman should be satisfied with a bullet that lands in the 22. There is no such thing as a wind of perfectly uniform velocity, but twelve inches of wind probably means anything from six inches to fifteen, neither will the most careful watching of flags avail much; beware of tinkering eternally with the windgauge, that is a fatal habit. Set it for about the average force and take what luck brings you.

Fishtail winds, that is those that vary from four o'clock around to eight are the most troublesome, and about all that can be done is to watch the flags and "hold for it" allowing the sight to remain at zero. Head winds, sweeping about from ten o'clock to two are also very vexatious, not only driving the bullet from side to side but down. Cuss the wind when it don't behave, but keep on holding close and it will get the other fellow's "goat" in place of yours.

Occasionally light will vary the elevation as much as six inches. An experienced marksman can usually give a pretty shrewd guess at the elevation before firing a shot, and a few "sighters" will tell him all he needs to know. As the sun descends usually the bullets will "drop" with it. If toward the finish of a good score the sun should become obscured by a passing cloud better wait till it clears before firing again.

The crack marksman must be of temperate habits. The man who smokes in order to keep his nerves steady will soon find himself betrayed by nervous irritability and the drinking man can only shoot well when braced up exactly so in which condition he finds it difficult to keep himself.

We might as well admit that success in match rifle work is entirely dependent on concentration of mind. Some men can concentrate powerfully but only for a very short time—they will make startlingly high scores but only now and then. Another will be able to keep to his knitting hour after hour, under any and all circumstances, and he is the man his club banks on in a match.

If ambitious to win and to break records, stuff cotton into your ears, smile when spoken to but never reply and never hear what is said. If the other end of the shooting house falls down and kills a man, never know it as long as your end is standing. Say nothing and saw wood, say nothing and saw wood; it is man killing work, but it gets results. WORK tells the whole story, for there is no fun about it, and it is not to be denied that concentration is the bane of all American sports.

The other way of match shooting is to take things as they come. Shoot only when you feel like it. Talk, listen, laugh, and watch the play. Rejoice with the man who made three reds in succession, and sympathize with the peppery old fellow that the dog-gone blinkity blanked marker is forever cheating by showing a ten where he held right for the dead center. Yes, the farce-comedy never was seen that could touch a German Schuetzenfest. But cheek by jowl with the fellowship and the humor comes the training that gives man dominion over the beasts of the field, makes his country impregnable, gives him a power of life and death only second to that of his Maker.

THE END

Books for Lovers of the Great Outdoors

The Outing Handbooks and a Specially Selected List of Travel, Biography and Fiction

Outing Handbooks, Each, Illustrated, 12°, $1.00

RIFLES AND RIFLE SHOOTING
By CHARLES ASKINS

WING AND TRAP SHOOTING
By CHARLES ASKINS

SPORTING FIREARMS
By HORACE KEPHART

PISTOL AND REVOLVER SHOOTING
By A. L. A. HIMMELWRIGHT

THE FINE ART OF FISHING
By SAMUEL G. CAMP

FISHING KITS AND EQUIPMENT
By SAMUEL G. CAMP

FISHING WITH FLOATING FLIES
By SAMUEL G. CAMP

FISHING TACKLE   By PERRY D. FRAZER

PRACTICAL BAIT CASTING
By LARRY ST. JOHN

AMATEUR RODMAKING
By PERRY D. FRAZER

SALT WATER GAME FISHING
By CHARLES F. HOLDER

EXERCISE AND HEALTH
By WOODS HUTCHINSON

BOXING   By D. C. HUTCHINSON

SWIMMING AND WATERMANSHIP
By L. DE B. H'ANDLEY

THE MACMILLAN COMPANY
Publishers   64–66 Fifth Avenue   New York

THE MACMILLAN COMPANY
Publishers 64-66 Fifth Avenue New York

Outing Handbooks (Continued)

THE MACMILLAN COMPANY
Publishers 64-66 Fifth Avenue New York

The Adventure Library

Edited by HORACE KEPHART

Specially Compiled for Sportsmen

Each 12°, $1.25

CAPTIVES AMONG THE INDIANS

CASTAWAYS AND CRUSOES

THE GOLD HUNTER
By J. D. BORTHWICK

HUNTING IN THE YELLOWSTONE
By EARL DUNRAVEN

THE LION HUNTER
By RONALYN GORDON-CUMMING

HOBART PASHA
By AUGUSTUS CHARLES HOBART-HAMPDEN

ADRIFT IN THE ARCTIC ICE PACK
By ELISHA KENT KANE

FIRST THROUGH THE GRAND CANYON
By MAJOR JOHN WESLEY POWELL

ADVENTURES IN MEXICO
By GEORGE FREDERICK RUXTON

IN THE OLD WEST
By GEORGE FREDERICK RUXTON

WILD LIFE IN THE ROCKY MOUNTAINS
By GEORGE FREDERICK RUXTON

THE MACMILLAN COMPANY
Publishers   64-66 Fifth Avenue   New York

Lightning Source UK Ltd.
Milton Keynes UK
UKOW06f1958300717
306339UK00006B/132/P